MILLENNIUM WOMEN

&

GENDER ASSASSINATION

THE PLOT TO DESTROY ALL THINGS MALE

K. B. Lewis

Millennium Women and Gender Assassination:
The Plot to Destroy all Things Male

http://www.kerryblewis.com

For more information contact :

Brimingstone Press
5301 Alpha Rd
Suite 80 #200
Dallas, TX 75240
http://www.brimingstone.press

Book and Cover design by *Brimingstone Writer Services*

ISBN: 978-0-578-69544-0

First Edition: June 2020

1 2 3 4 5 6 7 8 9 10

TABLE OF CONTENTS

FOREWORD

I graduated from Unilex College in San Francisco with a degree in Business. I've owned my own business since 1991. Over time I owned a couple of service-based businesses that placed me inside customers' homes. While inside the homes I would notice that there would be single women or mothers but with no man living with them.

It didn't matter the economic background (high income or low), it didn't matter the race, it didn't matter the neighbourhood. I asked the same question to each woman and they all gave me the same or similar answer. The question was, "Where is the man?" Then I would get the same answer almost verbatim. They all said, "I have my own house, my own car, my own money, I'm an independent woman and I don't need a man for anything." So, I thought to myself that that's no coincidence.

I then set out on this quest to research this situation because it so deeply affected my own personal experience. I talked to every woman in every house I went to, and every woman I encountered at the gym and even on the street. I talked to thousands of women over the years to conduct research for this book.

The thing that struck me most was that nobody had done any research on how women had come from being culturally dependent to becoming independent. This was a major paradigm shift and there needed to be more research on the effects of this change. I talked to and reviewed my work through several psychologists and relationship therapists, and I found out even they never heard of this paradigm shift.

I had a burning desire to get answers to my questions. One major thing that I discovered through my research from talking to thousands of women was that I found the three aspects of negative independence—selfishness, control, and competition—all of which contradict and neutralize the positive independence that we all hear independent women claim.

For almost over two decades, I have had intense discussions with thousands of women in relationships. Therefore, this book is based on WOMEN'S "OWN" STORIES—IN WOMEN'S "OWN" WORDS—FROM INDEPENDENT WOMEN "OWN" MOUTHS....

I've read countless books on relationships, on why they fall apart and how to fix them. I've talked to and discussed with numerous relationship experts and psychologists to get into the mindsets of independent women and men regarding relationships. I've had two failed marriages, both with independent women so I have walked the walk—I don't just talk the talk.

My life experience has qualified me as an expert on the

mentality of independent women's relationship issues and the paradigm shift that they have unknowingly created.

GENDER ASSASSINATION
Seek and destroy all things male
BATTLE OF THE SEXES taking advantage of being woman
A HOSTILE POWER GRAB Of
Emasculation by Intimidation

THE AGENDA—
MAKING MEN OBSOLETE
"If women are allowed to smear, vilify, tear down and damage the male gender as a whole, then they can take down every man in power and replace them with women-- which gives women TOTAL DOMINANCE over men and sole power and control-- Which means-- NO BALANCE- NO FAIRNESS & NO DUE PROCESS FOR MEN AKA #METOO!
Therefore Creating
A POWER GRAB by GENDER ASSASSINATION"

INTRODUCTION

WOMEN ARE—
STRONG-EQUAL-INDEPENDENT & VERY SERIOUS
COMPETITORS TO MEN— when it benefits them and
weak defenseless victim when it doesn't— WOMEN CAN
NO LONGER HAVE IT BOTH WAYS!
Women are either equal to men or they are NOT - THERE IS
NO IN BETWEEN!
WOMEN'S sense of ENTITLEMENT to disrespect, belittle
& abuse men
WOMEN Acting AS IF they are princesses on the throne who
can do NO wrong— who are ABOVE MEN, BEYOND
REPROACH—ENTITLED & UNTOUCHABLE

USING MALE SUPPRESSION TO MAKE MEN
UNEQUALLED
You can't dictate to me - I dictate to you
You can't talk to me that way because I'm a woman. In
other words — (I'm special, I deserve preferential treatment,

I'm supposed to have an advantage over men because I'm
entitled— I'm privileged— I'm better than you- and I'm
above you)
You can't criticize me
You can't judge me
You can't make me accountable for my actions
You can't challenge me
You can't debate me
You can't check me
You can't compete against me
You can't have an opinion opposing me
You can't disagree with me because it's sexist
You can't disrespect me (women) even if I disrespect you
(men)
You can't abuse me— even if I abused you first
You can't fight me back
You can't defend yourself against me
You can't look down on me
You can't talk negatively to me
You can't talk back to me
You can't tell me what to do
You can't give me any advice
You can't look at me sexually
You can't talk to me sexually
You can't say anything that I dislike
You just Do as I say—not as I Do!
What would happen if a man said these things to women?
It would be called a sexist- offensive- attack on all women-
(By women) -- But since it's a woman that saying it- -it's

called women's empowerment! --A Double standard!
UNEQUALLED—MENS EQUALITY REVOKED!

ARE WOMEN TRULY EQUAL TO MEN-- IF THEY
WANT SPECIAL PRIVILEGES AND PREFERENTIAL
TREATMENT OVER MEN FOR—"JUST BEING A
WOMAN"?
WOMEN ARE STRONG, EQUAL, INDEPENDENT &
VERY SERIOUS COMPETITORS TO MEN--
when it benefits them and weak defenseless victims when
it doesn't—
WOMEN CAN NO LONGER HAVE IT BOTH WAYS
WOMEN ARE EITHER EQUAL TO MEN OR
THEY'RE NOT? THERE IS NO IN BETWEEN!

THE SMEAR CAMPAIGN that NAMES - SHAMES
and BLAMES Everything that going wrong in HER life—
making it —HIS fault
Women GAINING AN ADVANTAGE Over men
By
GENDER INTIMIDATION

ENOUGH IS ENOUGH!
Men have a first amendment right to voice their opinions
and defend themselves just like strong independent women.
There is nothing wrong with that—It's a good thing for
women.

BUT MEN WILL NO LONGER BOW DOWN, GIVE
IN & GIVE A FREE PASS TO STRONG - EQUAL-
INDEPENDENT WOMEN, --WHO ARE VERY SERIOUS
COMPETITOR TO MEN!
THEY MUST STAND ON THEIR ON TWO FEET
AND HOLD THEIR OWN (JUST LIKE A MAN)
AND BE TRULY EQUAL (JUST LIKE THEY CLAIM
THEY ARE) -- & THAT MEANS--THEY HAVE TO TAKE
TO GOOD WITH THE BAD & THE POSITIVE WITH THE
NEGATIVE!
BECAUSE MEN WILL COMPETE BACK!
--BECAUSE- --
MEN COMPETING BACK --IS NOT AN ATTACK ON
WOMEN
MEN DEFENDING THEMSELVES -- IN NOT
OFFENSIVE &
MEN VOICING THEIR OPINIONS AND SPEAKING
THEIR MINDS --IS NOT SEXIST-- IT IS THEIR FIRST
AMENDMENT AMERICAN RIGHT!
And to all those who don't like it or who disagree with it I
say unto you—

"FRANKLY MY DEAR I DON'T GIVE A DAMN"

YOUR EXISTENCE AS A MAN IS UNDER ATTACK
AND IS IN SERIOUS AND IMMINENT DANGER!

MAN UP!

there's a target on your back

&

A PRICE TO PAY!

ARE YOU PREPARED TO PAY IT?

You have NO IDEA how much you don't know!

TAKING ADVANTAGE OF BEING A WOMAN:

"OFFENSIVENESS"
WOMEN'S WEAPON OF CHOICE

Women making everything an "OFFENSIVE-SEXIST ATTACK"!

Whether it's true or not- so that men can't challenge- oppose- check- debate or disagree with them in any way!

The Gateway and strong-arm tactics used to silence and censor men's voices and opinions in order to gain an advantage over them and empower themselves so that they can take full control and power in any given situation —

If women make anything and everything that they DISAGREE with or DISLIKE, offensive, sexist or an attack on all women, then they can censor, and silence men's voices and opinions at will. Therefore, they can go unchecked, unchallenged, unhinged and unbalanced. They can go unopposed into power with Total DOMINANCE!

That's Weaponizing sex and taking advantage of being a woman! That's how today's women have been empowering themselves over men!

BY SILENCING MEN
FOR BEING OFFENSIVE
FOR BEING A MAN!

Men—you can no longer allow women to use their gender to gain an advantage over you. Women are strong independent, equal and very serious competitors today and must be treated as such! That means that they can no longer claim to be a victim of an "offensive" attack in order to shut a man voice or opinions down in order to gain an advantage over them. Meaning—

WOMEN ARE—
STRONG-EQUAL-INDEPENDENT & VERY
SERIOUS COMPETITORS TO MEN— when it benefits
them and weak defenseless victim when it doesn't—

WOMEN CAN NO LONGER HAVE IT BOTH WAYS!
Women are either equal to men or they are NOT?
THERE IS NO IN BETWEEN!

WOMEN'S Since of ENTITLEMENT to disrespect-
belittle & abuse men.

WOMEN Acting AS IF they are PRINCESSES on the
throne who can do NO wrong— who are ABOVE MEN,
BEYOND REPROACH —ENTITLED & UNTOUCHABLE.

USING MALE SUPPRESSION TO MAKE MEN UNEQUALLED

You can't dictate to me - I dictate to you

You can't talk to me that way because I'm a woman. In other words— (I'm special, I deserve preferential treatment, I'm supposed to have an advantage over men because I'm entitled— I'm privileged— I'm better than you— and I'm above you)

You can't criticize me

You can't judge me

You can't make me accountable for my actions

You can't challenge me

You can't debate me

You can't check me

You can't compete against me

You can't have an opinion opposing me

You can't disagree with me because it's sexist

You can't disrespect me (a woman) even if I disrespect you (a man)

You can't abuse me— even if I abused you first

You can't fight me back

You can't defend yourself against me

You can't look down on me

You can't talk negatively to me

You can't talk back to me

You can't tell me what to do

You can't give me any advice

You can't look at me sexually

You can't talk to me sexually

You can't say anything that I dislike

You just Do as I say—not as I Do!

What would happen if a man said these things to women?

It would be called a sexist- offensive- attack on all women-

(By women) — But since it's a woman that saying it—it's

called women's empowerment! — A Double standard!

INEQUALITY— MENS EQUALITY REVOKED!

THAT'S TAKING ADVANTAGE OF BEING A

WOMAN!

WOMEN ARE—STRONG-EQUAL-INDEPENDENT &

VERY SERIOUS COMPETITORS TO MEN— when it

benefits them and the weak defenseless victim when it

doesn't—

WOMEN CAN NO LONGER HAVE IT BOTH WAYS!

Women are either equal to men or they are NOT! -

THERE IS NO IN BETWEEN!

WOMEN'S sense of ENTITLEMENT to disrespect-

belittle & abuse men.

WOMEN Acting AS IF they are PRINCESSES on the

throne who can do NO wrong— who are ABOVE MEN,

BEYOND REPROACH— ENTITLED & UNTOUCHABLE.

USING MALE SUPPRESSION TO MAKE MEN

UNEQUALLED

You can't dictate to me - I dictate to you

You can't talk to me that way because I'm a woman. In

other words — (I'm special, I deserve preferential treatment,

I'm supposed to have an advantage over men because I'm

entitled— I'm privileged— I'm better than you- and I'm

above you)

You can't criticize me

You can't judge me

You can't make me accountable for my actions

You can't challenge me

You can't debate me

You can't check me

You can't compete against me

You can't have an opinion opposing me

You can't disagree with me because it's sexist

You can't disrespect me (a woman) even if I disrespect you (a man)

You can't abuse me— even if I abused you first

You can't fight me back

You can't defend yourself against me

You can't look down on me

You can't talk negatively to me

You can't talk back to me

You can't tell me what to do

You can't give me any advice

You can't look at me sexually

You can't talk to me sexually

You can't say anything that I dislike

You just Do as I say—not as I Do!

What would happen if a man said these things to women? It would be called a sexist- offensive- attack on all women- (By women) -- But since it's a woman that saying it- -it's called women's empowerment! -- A Double standard! INEQUALITY— MENS EQUALITY REVOKED! THAT'S TAKING ADVANTAGE OF BEING A

WOMAN!

This is NOT an error or typo. I wrote this twice because I want you to get the full and complete understanding of how much of an advantage women have gained over men by silencing and censoring men's voices by making everything an "offensive" attack that women disagree with or dislike, while at the same time they have gone UNCHECKED, UNCHALLENGED, UNHINGED AND UNBALANCED! Meaning that men can't say anything negative to them without women saying it's an "offensive attack", even if they are just disagreeing or have an opposing opinion! That's how women have gain an advantage over men and empowered themselves.

Men—It's time to hold women accountable for their negative actions. Today's women are strong, independent, equal and very serious competitors to men and must be treated as such. Therefore, from this moment on if women claim an "offensive" attack for just a disagreement, debate, or challenge and so on. Push back and say——

"FRANKLY MY DEAR I DON'T GIVE A DAMN"!

Let it be known that you will NO longer allow strong, independent, equal women who are very serious competitors to men, use their gender as a victim card in order to gain an advantage over you anymore! She must stand on her on two feet and hold her own—just like the man who she claims to be equal to!

CHAPTER 1

"OFFENSIVENESS"

WOMEN'S WEAPON OF CHOICE and THE
PSYCHOLOGICAL CON-GAME That Women Play:
Strong, Equal and Independent (When it Favors them) and
Weak, Defenseless Victims (When it Favors them)!

Is the real reason that strong, independent women use the "offensiveness tactic" as a strategy to silence and censor men's voices and opinions because they can't measure up and compete head to head with strong independent men on a fair, balance and equal basis?

Men—women's emotions and sensitivity issues are a "weakness" that is used against you in order to gain your sympathy and an advantage over men to make it appear as if the big, strong, bad guy is beating up on and attacking a small defenseless, helpless, poor woman victim.

Women feel as if men should give them a break or a free pass for their weaknesses because that's how it has been done in the past when women were "dependent" upon men for emotional and economic support. However, now that this has changed and women have become strong, equal, independent, and very serious competitors to men in society today they still want men to keep them under that umbrella of needing sensitivity and emotional protection, while at the same time are competing against and defeating men with every opportunity they can because they are using that same weakness against men.

Today's women have intentionally tied men's hands behind their backs so that they can't fight back against women in any way or else it would be viewed an "offensive, sexist attack" on all women. today's women are the bullies and the victims at the same time. Today's women have developed passive-aggressive behaviors which causes them to bully men by taking the attitude that they can say or do whatever they want to a man with no consequences for their actions and at the same time claiming to be a victim of an offensive, sexist attack if men disagree, challenge, or oppose them in any way.

Today's independent women want it both ways but only when it favors them. Women claim that they are strong and can do anything that a man can do and even better. Right? But if that's the case then why are they claiming to be victims when men talk rough and tough like some men do? That means that they can't handle it or can compete on a man's level if they claim to be offended if a man talks tough to them.

If they can't emotionally handle what a man handles, then what makes them equal to men? That means that their emotions are a weakness if they claim that their feelings are hurt and are offended when a man says something they think is offensive to them, but at the same time they say the men have to have thick skin and need to suck it up and move on.

However this would mean that women are thin skinned and can't handle what a man can handle because the woman is claiming that her feelings are hurt and that she is offended for the same tough language that a man has to deal with on a daily basis. so, because women can't handle things as tough as men can, they then claim to be a victim of an offensive, sexist attack in order to cover up their weaknesses so that they don't have to admit that they are not equal, which would be an embarrassment to them so they deflect and call the men sexist or offensive and that way the focus is taken off of their short comings and all the blame is put on the men.

Women have been bragging and bolstering the idea that they are equal to men but now that's been unmasked and revealed that it's just not true. If it is, then why are they claiming to be offended because they can't handle tough talk like a man? Men have a right to speak their minds and compete with women. Just like women are doing with them. And if competing is an attack on women, (according to women) then wouldn't women competing against men be an offensive attack on men? What's the difference? Gender? Hmmm.

Men—remember that competing back with women is not an attack on women like they claim. in other words, women want men to just let them have their way when they compete against men but they don't want men to compete back and are trying to make men competing back an offensive attack on all women.

That's interesting because if women view men who compete with them as attacking them, under their theory aren't women who compete with men conducting an attack on men? In other words, women want the freedom to compete with men in all categories, and there is nothing wrong with that, but at same time these same women who are competing with men are saying that men shouldn't be able to compete back because that would be an offensive attack on women.

Get it now? What these women are saying is, just let us have your job, your house, your seat on the board, your political positions, etc, and if you try to stand up for yourself by competing back then you as a man are offensive and attacking women, so bow down and back away and let me have it or I as a woman will smear and destroy you. Get it now? This is how women have bullied their way into power.

Men—this is no accident. This is a strategic plan to make you timid, intimated, and afraid of women so that you won't stand up for yourself and allow women to have their way in any given situation, while at the same time you get nothing or you get smeared and destroyed. This is a strategic plan hatched by feminists and women's groups and has been passed down to the everyday average woman who now does the dirty work for the feminists and women's groups and now women's bullying has been disguised and wrapped up in the sensitivity and emotional cloth of "offensiveness", which is why they claim that they are "offended."

This gets men to bow down and back away therefore giving them what they want in any situation every time they dislike or disagree with men. This bullying tactic, or "offensiveness", has been disguised and normalized by women and it has emboldened them to the point that they now feel entitled!

Therefore, women's sense of entitlement is the true reasoning behind why they "feel" offended every time men say something that they disagree with or dislike. They "feel" and act as if they are an authority figure over men, like their mother or princesses on the throne who are better than and are above men and not equal to them, as if men are beneath them, here to serve them and are not on their level!

Meaning—"how dare you speak to the *princess* that way!" They believe consciously and subconsciously that men should put women on a pedestal because they are special, privileged, and deserve preferential treatment over them. Therefore, they think they are entitled to respect from men, and don't have to earn it like men have to (which is nature's law).

If you don't believe this or understand today's women's mentality, then let me enlighten you. If men and women are equal (as women claim) then why do they feel like they deserve respect for their gender without earning it? The only reason why women feel like they deserve respect for "just being a woman" is because they have a sense of entitlement. And if you feel that's not the case, then how do you explain this phenomenon?

No matter how you spin it or try to justify it, it's going to keep coming back to their sense of entitlement being the reason why they feel offended and disrespected for being a "woman". The "offensiveness" narrative is what's driving this movement to silence and censor men's voices so that women can gain an advantage and take power from men to empower themselves.

It's like two "competitive" football teams playing for the championship who get together and one team sets the rules (the women) for the other team (the men). The rules say that they (the women) can tackle you but you (the men) can't tackle them. So how do you keep them from scoring? You can't!

So, one team (the women) has all the power and totally dominates the other team (the men) and wins every time and the other team loses every time. Well, that's what women are doing to men when they make everything men say "offensive" to them in order to silence and censor their opinions and voices whether true or not.

Men can't tackle the women. In this example tackling women is men competing back, challenging, checking, debating and opposing them. Therefore, women are emboldened and empowered to bully men and push them around and kick them to the side like roadkill in order to take power in any given situation.

That's what taking advantage of being a woman means. This is what's going on in today's society and this is why men feel intimidated, frustrated, and powerless against women when they disagree or oppose them. This is why you feel less than a man, as if your manhood has been taken from you. because it has!

This is why you feel bullied, bulldozed and belittled. you are not crazy. You are right—and now it's time to do something about it and push back—by competing back! By letting women know that they will be held accountable for their negative actions. By challenging, debating, and speaking your mind and voicing your opinion. by letting women know that they can't use their gender as a crutch to intimidate and bully you anymore.

By letting them know that the "offensiveness" tactic will not work on you anymore in order to silence and censor you. by letting them know that they are strong, independent, equal and very serious competitors to men and that they have to stand on their own two feet just like the men whom they claim to be equal to.

And by letting them know that if they don't like or disagree with it then you will respectfully say—"frankly my dear I don't give a damn" and leave it at that! And do not *ever* apologize for being a man!!!

Men—you should not concern yourself with how a woman "feels" about any situation that has man versus a woman because she is using her emotions, feelings, and gender to gain advantage over you.

She is using her weakness and standpoint to gain sympathy in order to take you out of power, your job, economic and political positions in order to replace you, which leaves you S.O.L, meaning "shit out of luck!" and that's what taking advantage of being a woman is. She's looking to leave you hungry and homeless.

Today's women are strong, equal, independent, and very serious competitors to men and must be treated as such. there are more women working in today's society then men. This is a competitive world that we leave in. It's either you or her that's gets the job or promotion. It's either you or her who gets the house and puts food on the table.

Men—you can no longer allow a woman to use sympathy or her emotions to say that you are "offensive" in order to get the upper hand by silencing and censoring your voice or opinions and to push you out of a job or power. That's her taking advantage of being a woman. However, if you don't push back by competing back then you will get exactly what you deserve, which is nothing!

A woman will never allow a man to silence or censor her voice or opinion, so why should you? Men—have you forgotten that you are equal to them too? You don't have to stand by and let a woman tear down your manhood, silence your voice and opinions and to frustrate and destroy your life. You have First Amendment rights too! It's time to take a stand and compete back by pushing back.

Competing back is not "offensive", "sexist" or an "attack" on women. It's your right, duty and obligation to look out for your own best interests and protect yourself and your existence as a man! She's looking out for herself and doesn't give a damn if you succeed or fail, eat or starve, have a home or are homeless! So, you'd better be doing the same!

Stop allowing women (who are very serious competitors) to take advantage of you—by taking advantage of their being women! there is a saying—"be careful what you ask for because you just might get it." Women asked for equality and now they have it. Men—don't be scared to stand up for yourself against a strong, independent, and "equal" woman who is a very serious competitor.

Women are not victims. So, don't let them use the "offensiveness" tactic against you anymore to silence and censor your voice or opinions. Again, that's them taking advantage of their being a woman. And if they can't handle the truth, to stand on their own two feet, without using their emotions to get sympathy and gain an advantage over men, then that means that they are not equal to men.

That's using weakness and shows they are not as strong as they claim that they are—and that's them taking advantage of their being women! Now there are those of you who may say that I'm telling men to be mean or cruel to women by attacking women for being women. No, that's not what I'm saying.

The problem with feminists and women's groups is that they tell women that men who disagree or oppose women are *attacking* women. They tell women that it's offensive and sexist if men put up any resistance to them in their quest for power. The problem with this bad advice is that they make women feel and believe that they are entitled, and that they don't have to compete with men. They made women believe that men who compete against them are sexists, offensive and attack women.

Therefore, men shouldn't be able to compete and should just let women have their way and that's why women are offended. I know some of you may be saying that these men would put women out on the street with their children so this is why they need a helping hand or a hand up. Well, you are right, except that you may have forgotten that men have a wife and or significant other too, which they must take care of also.

So, why should a single woman or mother or any woman get a job or economic position over a man? They are not entitled to that job or position over him. Everyone and everything is supposed equal and fair game. Remember women chose to be independent and to compete with men for these jobs and now that they have to compete with men (which in itself is not offensive, sexist or an attack on women), they have to accept the disappointments.

They have to accept the good with the bad and the positives with the negatives. Men don't owe women anything anymore, and that includes breaks, a helping hand, preferential treatment, special privileges, a free pass, or any advantage. This is a dog-eat-dog world and women have *chosen* to dive into it headfirst by claiming independence.

There is that saying again—-"be careful what you ask for because you just might get it." Well, women have asked to be independent and now they have to deal with the real competition that comes along with it, and that includes competition from men. If they expect anything different then they are delusional because from this moment forward, there will be no more of taking advantage of their being women through their "offensiveness" tactics.

Men don't owe women anything and women are not entitled to power, a job or economic and political positions for just being women. they have to earn it just like the men! And for those who say that we as a society have to be sensitive to women's needs because they are emotional, then I ask, *why?*

Why do men have to be sensitive to women's needs when they are supposed to be strong, equal, independent, and very serious competitors to men. If men have to have compassion or be sympathetic to women's emotional needs, then that means that women are not as strong and as equal to men as they claim to be. Furthermore, it means that women are beneath men, and need special help BECAUSE THEY JUST CAN'T MEASURE UP TO MEN.

I know some of you are saying well, that's offensive. I ask, *why*? Women have changed the rules for how they want men to treat them (which is equally), but they still want men to remain in a traditional role when it comes to being treated by them like they are special and privileged, and with preferential treatment ("chivalry"). But at the same time, they want to compete with men, and try to defeat and destroy them with every opportunity and in every area that they can including economically and politically.

That's women taking advantage of their being women. By women claiming it's offensive if men don't treat them with sensitivity and sympathy because they are emotional, they are trying to use the "offensiveness" strategy and tactics in order to force men to bow down to their needs, wants and desires, which includes to silence and censor men's voices and opinions in order to gain an advantage and take power from them.

It's a hostile take down because women want to take away men's first amendment rights to freedom of speech, while at the say time expressing their own. Women want it both ways. This is how they have blindsided men and unfairly bent the rules to favor them and to empower themselves over men.

Men—-this is the reason why you have to push back and expose this "offensiveness" tactic and strategy because when women say that they are "offended" by you as a man, this is not an accident. This is a strategic tactic. using the "offensiveness" card is women's way of making themselves out to be the victims in order to gain sympathy from others.

By silencing and censoring men's voices and opinions, women get other women and some men to gang up on you in order to make it appear as if you are the bad guy who is beating up on this poor defenseless woman. It's a psychological con game by the women who use other people to support their cause—her side of the story and her point of view.

The strategy is to shame, belittle and bully you to comply to their needs and get whatever they want by pitting enough people against you so that you can't defend yourself or oppose her in any way, shape, form or fashion. This is how women have empowered themselves and defeated men and gained an advantage over men by silencing and censoring men's voices and opinions.

This strategic tactic of "offensiveness" is how women get the upper hand and grab power over you as men. Now, are there exceptions to these rules? Yes. But this is the rule because it's a strategic tactic and not the exception. Now—you as a man will have to walk around on eggshells and double check your language and every word you say in order to make sure that the average woman is not "offended" by you.

You have to ask permission to speak as if she is an authority figure over you, your mother, or a princess sitting on the throne who can do no wrong. Is this the woman who you are supposed to be "equal" to? Am I right? I guess not? In her eyes you're not worthy!

I'd like to know who died and put women in charge of men and took away men's first amendment rights to free speech by silencing and censoring men's voices and opinions? This "offensiveness" strategic tactic has taken away men's voices and opinions to the point where you as a man can't even be a man anymore!

Now—there are some men (not all) whom the feminists and women's groups have used and gotten to side with women and against their own best interests. these are men that come to the defense of the women like a knight in shining armor. These feminist sympathizers or so-called "protectors" truly believe that they are doing a good deed or supporting a good cause for the equality of women. These men that come to the rescue for women are actually harming and doing women a disservice.

You may ask, "why is that?" It's because these kind of men believe that women are weak and cannot measure up to or handle themselves head to head with a strong independent man. Therefore these "feminist sympathizers" are actually hurting women because they keep seeing women as weak and needing protection. They say that women are not equal to men therefore they need protection from strong independent men whom they can't compete against, therefore they will protect the women because today's women can't protect themselves since they are just not as capable as a man.

What they are saying by their definitive action of protecting women is that the women are too weak to handle a man's job, too sensitive, and emotional to handle a man's rough and tough language, and too weak to handle challenging situations on her own. These "feminist sympathizers" are saying that women are not equal to them, like children and that they are not strong enough to handle a man's conversation. therefore, they think they need protection from this and that they are the ones to protect the women, since women are too weak to protect themselves.

If a woman claims that she is offended by a man then that means that she is not equal to a man (according to these "feminist sympathizers") and we as a society have to take away men's first amendment rights to free speech in order to protect these poor fragile women (who may break if they get seriously challenged by a strong man) from the big bad man talk.

This is what these "feminist sympathizing" men, feminists and women and women's groups are saying to men. Again—these people believe they need to take away men's First Amendment rights to free speech thru silencing and censoring their voices just because women can't handle tough talk like a man can. But I thought women were supposed to be strong, equal, independent and very serious competitors to men? One asks.

I guess they are not as strong and as equal to men like they claim to be if they can't handle a challenge from a strong man. And if that's the case then they are actually inferior to men and therefore men are superior to women, because men handle women's tough talk all the time (uncensored).

That's if they are offended by tough talk by men. and if that's not the case then why do women say that men's tough talk is offensive and want to violate men's first amendment rights by silencing and censoring them for tough talk? Women can't have it both ways. Either women are strong and can handle tough talk like a man or they are weak victims and can't handle tough talk from men. There is no in between!

Women wanting to have it both ways are taking advantage of their being women. By the way—the special beauty of free speech is that although you may not like what is said, you disagree with it or you may be offended by it, but all Americans have a right to say it, and nobody can take this right away from men, including women!

I know some of you will say that those comments that women are beneath men and men are superior to women are offensive and sexist. I'm not saying that that is the case. I'm just asking the question—"is it true?" Because if the answer is "no," since women are equal to men and not inferior— then why are women offended and can't handle tough language from men like men handle tough language from women?

And if the answer is "yes"—that women can handle tough language from men—and are not beneath men and men are not superior to women—then why do they want to silence and censor men's voices and opinions for being "offensive", but they don't want women's voices or opinions silenced and censored when they offend men?

The freedom of speech is guaranteed by our Constitution, whether you agree with it or not. However, these same men (the "feminist sympathizers") believe that if they just go along with the feminists' agenda then they would be looked at favorably by women and that they would be liked more than the more masculine men whom they disagree with on almost every issue. then they can somehow get on the women's good side and then the women would not see them as being "sexist", "offensive", or "attacking", women.

These delusional men believe that they would be liked, or get sex, or some other kind of favorable treatment from women and feminists if they just opposed other men with self-deification. what these men don't understand is that once they leave the room and the women's presence, everything that they were against with the other men who they helped demonize, now applies to them!

In other words, they are now the same villain that they helped to villainize. They are now the bad guys now that they are out of the women's presence. They are now the "offensive sexists" who are attacking women. What these weak men (the "feminist sympathizers") don't understand is that appeasement is not their friend, it's their enemy because now they are the toxic masculine men that the feminists and women's groups have demonized and hate.

Therefore, their attempts at appeasement and being naive have only emboldened these women and justifies their bullying cause and princess like behavior. Which is taking advantage of being a woman. This kind of men have been so intimidated and bullied to the point where they are afraid to speak up or defend themselves against a woman, even if she is wrong and he is right!

The reason these men are so afraid to voice their opinions is because the feminists and the women's groups have made it so that any man that says anything that's opposing or appears as if it's attacking women is viewed as attacking on all women. Whether this is true or not.

Let me say that again because this is essential, and it's the gateway and underline bullying tactic used to intimidate men into submission and get their way, and to get men to bow down and surrender to the feminist agenda! The agenda which is the taking advantage of being a woman.

By turning the tables and using reverse psychology (on these men who fell for the con game) they are making it appear as if the women are the ones being attacked by men, when in actuality it's the women who are attacking the men. This "smoke and mirrors" tactic is an optical illusion.

Here's what I mean—if women can get men to focus on their so-called attacks on women then the men stop focusing on the women who are actually attacking them. this is called "deflection" and a "bait-and-switch". They attack the men first then once he tries to defended himself, then the woman will say that he "attacked" her by his disagreeing with or opposing her, which makes it appear as if he is trying to stop her from achieving her goals.

Now, from this point forward the men will stop opposing or disagreeing with women because he doesn't want to come across as sexist. get it now? In other words she got him to bow down and fight for her cause with her against other men (which goes against his own best interests as a man) because she has made him believe that opposing or disagreeing with her is sexist, and not just a simple disagreement.

Therefore, women get to go unchecked and unchallenged into power with the help of some "feminist sympathizer" men using a psychological con game. This strategy is also known as "divide and conquer". Think about it. if women can get half the men on their side against the other half of men in society then it's game over for all men! And this includes the feminist sympathizers and appeasers.

There will be no fairness or balance to halt your demise as a man. That's what taking advantage of being a woman is! This is where the feminists in this country are going and you'd better wake up (if you are man) now, before it's too late! They are more than halfway to their goal now! Haven't you noticed? if not, just take a look around you and tell me if you don't have to walk around on eggshells and double check what you say to a woman today?

Tell me if you just verbally disagree with a woman that she won't look at you as if you just offended her. As if she is entitled and above you like a princess?

Tell me if you can speak your mind without a woman opposing you? Tell me if you can make a negative comment to a woman without her trying to silence and censor your voice and opinions, yet she can make all the negative comments about you that she wants with no consequences because as a man you fear that you would be smeared and demonized as an "offensive sexist" who is attacking women.

Am I right? That's the psychological con game women use against men, and that's what's going on in today's society. That's women taking advantage of being women.
Offensiveness is like beauty, it's in the eye of the beholder. If a woman says that she is offended by what a man says but at the same time the man says that he is offended by what the woman says to him, then whose offensiveness trumps the other and why?

I'm sure that most of you would say the woman because women are more sensitive and emotional than men. Right? however, this just proves my point that women feel like they are entitled to preferential and special treatment *just because they are women*. Also, this would be saying that women are weaker than men and not equal to men because they need some kind of help just to cope with the problems that men have to face on a daily basis which in turn means that women are inferior to men.

They need a helping hand because they can't deal with their emotions like a man can and just suck it up and deal with criticism and move on like we tell men to do when they are offended by something that they didn't like. So now that we are equal, now it's time for women to suck it up just like they have told men to do since the beginning of time or else they just must admit that they are not equal because they just can't handle the same things or solve problems like a man can.

This is why they use "offensiveness" tactics in order to help them silence, censor and control men from exposing them and to cover up their own weaknesses, faults, flaws, and short comings, WHICH CAUSE THEM TO NOT MEASURE UP TO MEN. However if you are prone to, or looking to take offense to everything (which the feminists and women's groups have conditioned and brainwashed most women to do) then I'm sure that you hear offensiveness in these statements rather than women taking advantage of being women. Which proves my point!

Let me give you an example of a psychological con game so that you will understand what it is and how it looks. in January of 2020, in the Democratic Party debate on CNN, Presidential Candidate Senator Elizabeth Warren (a woman) accused Senator Bernie Sanders (a man), who is also running for president, of sexism.

Senator Warren was slipping in the polls right before the Iowa caucuses and Senator Sanders was gaining momentum and was leading in the polls. Senator Warren told the press that one of her staffers heard from someone who heard from another staffer that Senator Sanders said in 2018 that a woman can't be president of the United States.

Remember now, this was two years ago and the staffer whom she claimed told her this two years ago wasn't in the room and claimed that they had heard it from someone else. So, it was hearsay on top of hearsay, which means nobody knows if it was true or not and senator sanders denied it.

However, that didn't stop Senator Warren from using it to smear her male opponent and label him a sexist with this derogatory unchecked and unverified statement. So now Senator Warren got the press to ask a question to every Presidential Candidate and the American people— "do you believe that a woman can be president?"

And there can only be one answer and that answer better be "yes" otherwise you would be called and labeled a "sexist". Now, nobody knows if the smear was true or not, but that wasn't point. The point was to intimidate Senator Sanders and men in general and to get the American people to start talking about a woman becoming president so that senator warren can get pass the stigma and break the glass ceiling so that women can be president and then capture the women's vote by getting them angry and riled up against the men.

All this in order to get the vote for a woman candidate and not a man and Senator Sanders was just collateral damage along the way. So Senator Warren used a psychological con job (offensiveness and sexism) in order to halt and take down senator sanders by using a strawman to get women offended and label a powerful man as a sexist without one strand of proof or evidence that he said or made the derogatory comment.

A strawman is a made up, illusional story that doesn't exist and is used as if it is true in order to get women "offended" at something that was never true in the first place.

Get the psychological con game now? That's women taking advantage of being women. Now Senator Warren can go out and campaign on being a woman who was a victim of a sexist attack by a male opponent (which we know is a lie!) based on a made-up story that nobody could verify.

Therefore, she is able to get the women on her side and against the men in order to get votes for her instead of the men. Get the con game now? She used sexism as a weapon to get women "offended" so that they would stand against men and side with her. This is an example of a woman initiating a hostile take down by intimidation and bullying her way into power. That's a woman taking advantage of being a woman!

Has the thought ever crossed the minds of the "offensiveness crowd" and Senator Warren's own mind that perhaps she just isn't a good candidate and the lack of support for her in the polls wasn't sexism? But then again, it's not about actual offensiveness, it's about using the "offensiveness tactic" as a strategy to intimidate, bully, tear down, smear, censor, and silence men in order to take them down and gain power for women.

Now—I have no problem with women in power. But to gain that power by weaponizing their sex and lies will no longer be tolerated. It will be met, from this point forward—with resistance. Because these lies and smears upon the male gender as a whole cannot and will not go unchecked and unchallenged anymore by men!

Women who are tearing men down by weaponizing their sex, being dishonest, using intimidation and bully tactics, will be called out for what they are, and they will be met with force by men from this point on. Enough with the smears! Enough with the lies!

Enough with weaponizing sex—enough with women getting away with things by using the psychological con game of "offensiveness" as a strategy to destroy men's lives so that they can take power for themselves. and enough taking advantage of being a woman! —And to all those who think these comments are sexist, offensive and an attack on women, I say unto you: your tactics will not work anymore because those tactics have been exposed for what they are (which is complete bull!) and to all those who don't like or disagree with this—now you know how men feel when you bully, intimidate smear and tear them down!

So, "frankly, my dear, I don't give a damn" if you are offended because the psychological con game is over!

Men—the walls are closing in on you! It's now or never to stand up and fight for your equality and right to exist as a man! What are you going to do? Fight or surrender? The choice is yours! It's time for men to unite and stop the division among them and stop the demise of men's rights and the equality of women, by their taking advantage of being women.

Therefore men—-be aware of the psychological con game (offensiveness) that women use to get you to bow down to them, silence and censor your voice and opinions, because it gets you to go against your own best interests.

Get it now? Don't be fooled by this psychological con game used by women and that the feminists and women's groups have taught the women in your lives. This is their taking advantage of men and women by using women to do their dirty work for the feminists and women's groups in order to gain power in a hostile takeover.

Which is also known as women taking advantage of being women.

CHAPTER 2

TAKING ADVANTAGE OF BEING A WOMAN

"THE ENTITLED PRINCESS"

It doesn't matter what a woman does—MEN SHOULD JUST SHUT UP AND TAKE THE PUNISHMENT!

NO MORE TAKING ADVANTAGE OF BEING A WOMAN!

In this country society has given women special privileges of respect, meaning, that men don't shouldn't talk to women in a disrespectful way or abuse women or else there will be consequences and repercussions for their actions. We as a society will defend these protections for women. Why?

Because society in the past had viewed women as the weaker gender. Therefore, women were in need of protection from unruly men who would take advantage of them mentally and physically.

However, in today's society this view of weakness is past history. Why? Because today's women are strong, independent and equal to men and very serious competitors in every way, with a few minor exceptions. This is according to women. Women can speak their minds and voice their opinions without any censorship from men.

Today's women are very serious competitors to men. Today's women are very serious competitors to men. Today's women are very serious competitors to men.

Stop!

Before you think that I just made a typo or an error in editing, by making that statement three times, that is not the case. I meant to say that phrase three times in order to get your attention as to the specific point that I'm making.

Now, here is the problem for men and the challenge for women which they both now face. Women say that they want equality, except for when it comes to men's equality. The majority of women don't want men to challenge them.

Women don't want men to talk to them in a disrespectful way like they talk to men in a disrespectful way. Women don't want men to physically abuse them like they physically abuse men. You're probably saying, what do you mean by women abusing men? Men are the abusers.

Okay, here's what I mean. When a woman physically assaults or abuses a man first, and then the man retaliates or defend himself against that woman's attack, 99.999 % of women will say that "a man shouldn't hit a woman no matter what she does".

Right?

That statement alone makes my point that women don't want men to be equal and do what women do to them, which is to physically abuse them. That statement acknowledges that the woman did something wrong to the man by attacking or assaulting him first, however the woman doesn't want to be retaliated upon by the man, because she believes that he could seriously hurt or injure her if he hit her back.

Women also don't want men to verbally abuse them the way they verbally abuse men. Today's women are very strong, independent and serious competitors to men in our society. However, if that is the case then why are women still under this umbrella of protection and sense of entitlement regarding weakness when it comes to respect and abuse?

Today's women are no longer mentally weaker than men. They are no longer dependent upon men. They are financially independent. They are politically independent. They are equal to men in every positive way. However, today's women are also equal to men in a negative way too, and there lies the conflict and the problem.

Today's women are very disrespectful and abusive towards men to the point where men are afraid to engage or challenge them due the backlash that they might receive, because many women will disrespect, intimidate, publicly shame and bully them, and because they know and understand that men can't fight them back without some kind of consequence.

Women do all this in order to gain an advantage over men in any possible way that the they can or see fit. Therefore, if women are equal to men in a negative way as well, why then are women still under this umbrella of "respect" in order to protect them when they are doing equally as wrong as the men?

Why do women deserve respect from men, just for being women, when it hasn't been earned? That sounds a little sexist to me. Why? Because the respect given to women is solely based on her gender, and not the fact that she earned it with her actions or attitude or that it is deserved. Remember that women are profoundly serious competitors to men in every way including negatively.

Today's women have gone unchecked, unchallenged, unbalanced to the point where some women (but not all) are unhinged and they receive no consequences for their negative actions or behavior. If women can't handle what they dish out, then they shouldn't dish out negative behavior, and if women can't or won't do it, then we as a society need to rescind or take back the entitlement of "respect" that they have enjoy for decades and centuries.

Meaning that women can no longer expect to do wrong, be very disrespectful, intimidate and bully men and then hide or jump behind the gender card for the protection of "respect". Meaning the argument of "Don't talk to me in that way or disrespect me because I'm a woman." There lies the sense of entitlement and "taking advantage of being a woman".

What does "taking advantage of being a woman mean"? I know some of you may be thinking that that's some kind of derogatory comment towards women. Like sexism. Wrong, that's not true.

Most women talk nasty, disrespectful, and spit their trash and their bullshit at men in order to intimidate, and bully them in order to control them or the situation, because they know that they can jump behind the gender card for protection, and that there is nothing the men can do about it, because they will either get fired from their jobs for disrespecting and being offensive to women or go to jail for assaulting or attacking women.

Therefore, women get a free pass to attack men with no retaliation, punishment, consequences or repercussions for their bad actions or negative behavior. Which is solely based on their gender and being a woman. Therefore, these women are now emboldened to take advantage of their gender because it gives them great power over the men in their lives.

That's taking advantage of being a woman. However, it's a double edge sword because if a man retaliates, then it makes the woman look weaker than the man, which doesn't make sense because women said that they were strong independent and equal to men. Was that just B.S.? Or are women taking advantage of being a woman, using their gender to take advantage of their perceived weaknesses? Hmmm?

Example: it's like a pregnant woman, who is very aggressive and verbally abusive towards men and women. She is given a free pass and is allowed to be abusive to a certain point because we as a society don't won't any harm to come to her or her unborn child because she is at a weak point in her life.

The key word here is "weak". Therefore, she is given a free

pass to be abusive without consequence because of her sympathetic situation (i.e. with the baby) so therefore she is taking advantage of her being pregnant.

However, it's the same or similar situation in what today's women are doing with men. We as a society don't want to see a man abuse a woman physically or verbally so therefore the women are given a free pass because they are perceived to be the "weaker" sex or gender therefore women are given a break or free pass to be abusive or disrespectful towards men (to a certain point) without any retaliation, just like that pregnant woman, without any repercussions for their bad behavior.

Therefore, the women are emboldened by not getting punished for their aggressive, disrespectful, abusive and or negative behavior which mean that the women are take advantage of being a woman, because of their perceived "weakness" as women. In this case their "gender" is their perceived weakness. According to the women themselves. And if that's not the case then why do women want "respect" for just being "women" and not their earned value? I know some women will say that they want the earned respect too.

However, they still want respect for being a "woman", because it affords them the respect for being the "weaker gender". They want it both ways. They want the strength when it favors them, and there's nothing wrong with that, however they want the "weakness" when it favors them also. Which is where they are taking advantage of being a woman.

Many women take advantage of men because they know that men won't fight back because it makes them look bad and it will appear as if they are attacking a poor, weak, defenseless woman. So now these women are emboldened and proceed to talk a little rougher, tougher and more disrespectful towards men than they normally would because they know that there is nothing the men will do about it. And if he does retaliate, then they know that he would be punished in some way for his actions.

Therefore, they know they can get away with it. Some of them are very disrespectful to men but at the same time they don't want men to disrespect them. That's what taking advantage of being a woman is. They know that men can't disrespect women back because there will be some kind of negative consequence against them for doing so.

When a woman knows that a man on the job can't fight back or defend himself from her physically abusive attacks, like hitting him, slapping him, kicking him, spitting on him, verbally assaulting him and so on. That's what taking advantage of being a woman is.

Why does she do this? Because she knows that he will be severally punished for his actions if he retaliates. Women get more aggressive towards men in the workplace and try to bully them in order get their way, or get something that they want, knowing that the men can't fight back because it appears as if they are intimidating, bullying, verbally or physically attacking women, when in fact it is the women who are attacking them. That's what taking advantage of being a woman is.

Let me give you some examples of things that I have seen and heard from men and women that best describes, "taking advantage of being a woman".

I talked to a woman who once told me that she likes seeing

a man cow and bow down when she talks to him aggressively. This woman had told me that there was this guy on her job that she didn't like. She said that he was very arrogant, and that he always acted like he knew everything. So, every time she saw him and engaged him in a conversation, she would bring up the topic of sexism with him. She would say things like "men are pigs all they want is sex from women."

She said that she would say these things just to get a reaction out of him so that he would try to defend himself. She said that "she couldn't wait on him to say something so that I can shut him down and shut him up and put him in his place".

She said that soon as a word came out of his mouth that she would get loud so that everyone could hear her and then he would stop talking and look around to see if anyone heard them. Then she would say things like "you are just like those other men", "a pig" and when he would try to defend himself, she said that she would intimidate him and say things like, "you are such a guy."

She said that she would do those things, and talk to him in that way because she just wanted to see him bow down to a woman and because she knew that he couldn't talk back to a woman in the same way that she talked to him or if he did she would report him to management and possibly get him fired.

She said that she was purposely being a bitch to him because women have the power now and "men have to sit back and take their shit."

Now listen to what she said. She said that she talk aggressively towards him and called him names because "she knew that he couldn't talk back to her in the same way that she talked to him because she was a woman". If that's not (taking advantage of being a woman) then I don't know what is?

Another example is the New York Times lead technology writer Sarah Jeong. Here is an example of one of her tweets:

"Oh man it's kind of sick how much joy I get out of being cruel to old white men."

Now why did she say that, and why did she believe that she could get away with being "cruel" to old white men, when she is a young Asian woman? There could be several reasons for why she did this, but there's only one answer to why she believed that she could get away with it, and that's because she knew that old white men couldn't fight her back verbally or physically because that man would get fired for appearing as if they were attacking a small defenseless Asian woman, when in fact it was she who was the bully.

She was taking advantage of her being a woman. Their taking advantage of being women is the price that women believe that men should pay for having power over women, even if the man is rightfully in the power position, such as if he is her boss or manager. Some women believe that men shouldn't have any power over them, even if the men were put in charge over them on the job or at the workplace, and that's why they treat men with such disrespect.

When women take advantage of being a woman, what they are trying to do is make men irrelevant, and punish them, and put them behind and beneath women, so that the women can feel and believe that they are empowered. This is one of women's version of empowerment. It is considered empowering for women to dominate anything over a man even if that thing is bullying men.

You don't believe it? Then explain why many women, in most of the time (not all, of course) will try to get a man into a competition to defeat him in any situation. Why is this? It's because if they win or defeat him then they will feel empowered. If you haven't noticed there is always a competition, man vs. woman somewhere.

Why? So that women can prove themselves to be just as good as or better than a man. Why? Because this puts women on equal ground with men and that makes them feel empowered. Believe it or not.

The other ways of seeking empowerment are how they use other women's personal achievements and accomplishments as their own. Many times they combine them collectively as if they are one, as if they accomplished the same thing without doing the work individually, for solely being part of the same gender, as if their identification as a woman achieves the accomplishments and not their individuality. That is because they don't won't men to know about the sense of entitlement which they enjoy from their "taking advantage of being a woman".

If you don't believe this then explain why a woman would she get into a man's face, who is twice her weight and size and try to intimidate and bully him, knowing that she can't overpower him physically? It is only because she knows that he can't fight her back physically or else he will be punished in some way or go to jail. Therefore, she is taking advantage of her being a woman.

Why would a woman disrespect and loud talk and try to intimidate a man on the job? It's because she knows that he can't do the same thing to her. Which means that she will go unchecked by him, and when she is unchecked then she becomes unchallenged, which gives her a free pass to become unhinged in order to bully her way to power and promotion or whatever the goal is that she is trying to achieve, which also means that she can get control over him, and breaks the balance between men and women. So, she is taking advantage of her being a woman.

Here are other examples. A guy once confided in me and said that he was once in a domestic violence situation. He said that he and his girlfriend had gotten into a heated argument that quickly went wrong. I asked, "what happened?" He said that they were arguing and they both called each other some nasty names and she didn't like what he said about her and then she got aggressive and violent and hit him with her fist.

At first, he just shrugged it off, but then they continued to argue. However, when she saw that her punches didn't affect him, she proceeded to hit him again and again. This time she didn't stop. So, he put his hands up to block the punches, but she wouldn't stop. He tried to leave but when he turned his back on her she hit him in back of the head.

At that point he said that he got upset because he tried to walk away but she continued to assault him. He then said to himself, enough is enough because she was really trying hurt him and do some damage to him. So, at this point he had grabbed her hands and told her to stop. But she didn't stop. He said that his only choice at that point was to defend himself before he got seriously hurt.

So, he pushed her down to the ground and left. However, when he can back home later, he learned she had called the police on him and had him charged with assault. The charges were eventually dropped because she admitted that she had been the aggressor. Weeks later after everything had settled and he talked to her, he asked her why she called the police on him. She told him that it didn't matter what she did as a woman, a man still shouldn't put his hand on a woman because he is bigger and stronger than her.

He was dumbfounded and so was I. Now this case had me flabbergasted because I was asking myself what was he supposed to do in that situation? He did everything right. He tried to walk away but she kept coming at and hitting him. To him he had no choice but to protect himself.

Now this is a classic case of "taking advantage of being a woman". How so? Because she was the aggressor and the abuser in this case. She then used the excuse of being a woman in order to justify calling the police to have him arrested. Even though she hit him continuously and wouldn't stop, she made the gender bias case that, "it doesn't matter what a woman does" to justify her behavior.

Let me say that again so that everyone can understand. "It doesn't matter what a woman does to a man, he should just take the punishment and walk away". Let that sink in for a minute. This means she can do whatever she wants to him and there is absolutely nothing he can do about but take it. This is what she is saying here.

Wow! Really? If you didn't get my point before, I hope you get it now. It can't get any clearer than that. This is a textbook case of a woman "taking advantage of her being a woman".

I'm going to say this one more time to let it sink into your head. She believes that she is entitled to do bodily harm to a man, and he is supposed to just take her violent assault just because she is a woman. Unbelievable. This is the clear definition of her "taking advantage of her being a woman." No doubt. Get it now?

If you don't, then let me give you one more example. I talked to another guy who told me that he was having consensual sex with a woman and in the middle of having sex the woman had mumbled the words "stop" but he didn't hear her. Then she said it again but louder, then he stopped having sex with her and asked her what's wrong?

She was upset, and said I told you to "stop" he said, "I did." She said, "yeah but you did not stop the first I told you to stop." He said, "I didn't hear you the first time, but I stopped when I heard you clearly say 'stop'." She said "it didn't matter the second time because I told you the first time and you didn't stop. You raped me!" she said.

He replied and said, "what the hell are you talking about, I didn't rape you, you're crazy." Then she said, "no means no!" And they went back and forth on the issue and then he got up and left. The next day he got a knock on his door and it was the police. They asked what happened and he gave his side of the story.

He told them that it was consensual sex and that she mumbled something, but he didn't hear it clearly. He made it clear, however, when he did hear her say "stop" clearly, he stopped. He asked one of the officers, "how is that rape if I didn't hear or understand her?" They took him to jail anyway, but he later got out because her family and his family got together and got her to drop the charges because it was a misunderstanding.

Now you might be asking yourself how this is an example of her "taking advantage of her being a woman?" Here is how. She knew that she had the power to lock him up, and even though she knew it was a misunderstanding she did it anyway. She used her being a woman to justify having him locked up. She knew that the law would favor her and that he would have to prove that he didn't rape her. Which is backwards because she is the one that has to prove that he raped her.

However, by knowing that the law would favor her and put him in jail based on her word and not his word, she took advantage of her being a woman. Only when he called her crazy and then left, did she call the police. She was more upset about him calling her crazy, than she was about the so-called rape. This shows she use her power as a woman to have him locked up because she was angry at him, not for the so-called rape, but for the disrespectful attitude that he displayed towards her.

Therefore, she was "taking advantage of her being a woman."

Women are supposed to be strong independent and equal to a man in every way. They are supposed to be serious competitors, right? So why are so many women using the gender card to get ahead of men? The gender card of choice is their "taking advantage of being a woman" which has flown under the radar so far, until now! Most men don't have a clue that this tactic has been used against them in order to empower women.

However now this hidden weapon has now been exposed and uncovered. Men——from this point forward it's time to put a check, a challenge and a balance on women. Why? Because women are very serious competitors to men in the workplace and society today and they are equal to a man in every way, (according to them) so they can no longer be treated with "kid gloves", as if women were weak and NOT equal to men because they can't handle the situation like a man.

Or they need special treatment so that they can cope with the problem or situation because they can't handle it emotionally. They have to stand on their own two feet and stop using the crutches of their gender to empower themselves over men, which is what taking advantage of them being a woman is!

CHAPTER 3

WEAPONIZING SEX

WAS THE #ME TOO MOVEMENT CREATED IN
ORDER TAKE DOWN MEN IN POWER?

The #MeToo Movement vs #WeToo Movement:

Weaponizing sex sexual assault and harassment:

It's a Power Grab:

Male suppression:

What is weaponizing sex?

Weaponizing sex is when a woman uses sex to hurt,
dominate, tear down, destroy, take away, manipulate, shame,

intimidate, bully, and so on in order to gain an advantage over the men in their lives.

The #MeToo Movement

Let's start backwards and work our way forward. That is what the #MeToo movement and these women are advocating for. They are saying that they can go back into time, find a crime, and then go back to the future and have the men charged and prosecuted for that crime. A crime that the men can't prove that they didn't do! Let me say that again so that you can really understand and absorb what the ##MeToo Movement is all about. Read it again and again. So that you get the correct understanding of it.

They are saying that they can go back into time and then back into the future and have men charged with a crime, that that the men can't prove that they didn't do! In other words the women don't have to prove that something happened to them, (because they have no proof or evidence to back up their claims, only their word) they are saying that the men have to prove that they didn't commit the crime.

Wow, that's simply amazing! How can the men prove that? They can't and these women known that the men can't prove it. In other words, the men are guilty of the crime (from the women's point of view) because the men can't prove that they didn't do it! Unbelievable! Get it now? That's weaponizing sex!

What more do these women want?

Do they want to fix the flux capacitor in the DeLorean and

go back to the future and find Marty, Doc and George McFly and then have him charged with being a peeping tom and sexual harassment, for looking into Lorraine's window? If this concept wasn't so serious, I would think it was a joke! I would say, "wow, are you kidding me?"

This would make absolutely no sense, and if it makes no sense then it's not true. Now let me tell you what the "MeToo" Movement is really about, and what's really behind the curtains and underneath the rocks.

It's a power grab. Why would a woman want to go back ten, twenty, and even thirty years to seek justice or revenge on a man for a crime that neither one of them can prove happened? I'll tell you why: it's because it is not about justice. This is about a power grab. A power grab to bring powerful men down and replace those men with women. The feminists and the women's groups are behind this nefarious movement.

What they are trying to do is create an atmosphere and a change of culture to make it so that they can use a woman's so call sexual assault or harassment cases as a weapon in order to bring down powerful men anytime they want, especially when there is a political or powerful position they are interested in pursuing. They want to use the old past sexual assault cases in order to make it okay for them to bypass men's due process rights and tear down the burden of proof, so that they can weaponize sex and use it in the present day in order to bring down the men in power today.

It's a dirty underlying and hidden agenda and war on men that these women are waging in order to gain power. Think about it. If a woman can say that a man sexually assaulted her, without one strand of proof or evidence, then it makes her the most powerful woman on earth. Why? Think about it! Accusing a man of sexual assault is the most powerful nefarious weapon that a woman can use against any man should she succeed in her quest.

Sexual assault can bring down an empire. It can bring down a C.E.O of a large corporation. Sexual assault can bring down a congressman, a senator, a president, and even a Supreme Court justice, which is probably more powerful than the president of the United States because this is the person who has the last word when it comes to confirming our laws, like abortion rights.

Don't believe it? This is exactly the case and what happened in the 2018 Supreme Court hearings with Justice Brett Kavanaugh. The political left-wing feminists joined up with the #MeToo Movement and used a woman named Dr. Christine Blasey Ford to help push their agenda to weaponize sex in order to block a Supreme Court justice nomination.

Remember that Dr. Ford didn't want to come forward with this case. The feminists, of which senator Diana Feinstein is one of them, purposely leaked Dr. Fords case to the media in order to draw attention to a possible problem for Judge Kavanaugh. The #MeToo Movement and the feminists knew that a sexual assault case would definitely be a problem and possibly could derail the nomination of Kavanaugh.

Therefore, they brought to the forefront a thirty-five-year-old sexual assault case in an attempt to stop the nomination of Judge Kavanaugh. Remember the accuser, Dr. Ford, had zero evidence or proof that Judge Kavanaugh committed this crime of sexual assault against her. She had no proof of not only that a sexual assault didn't take place, but she also had no proof that she even knew Brett Kavanaugh.

Despite all this, this circus was still tried on the floor of the senate while the world watched. Ford's answers were evasive, and she got caught in several lies and her lawyers were advocates of feminist groups. There was a clear agenda here, and it was evident. You could see right through it. The #MeToo Movement is a gateway to the road to intimidate men and tear men down and get them out of powerful positions so that they can be replaced by women. It's a total power grab, and the feminists are using women to accomplish their agenda. This is clearly weaponizing sex!

The easiest way to grab power from a man and transfer it over to women is to accuse him of sexual assault. Even if the man is innocent his name and his reputation will be marred because they will be smeared and dragged through the mud in public view and there will always be doubt about him in the people's eyes.

Therefore, the man would have to resign from a position of power or become an advocate for women's groups. Which means, he could help them advance their agenda for them. Either way the feminist women will win. Now there are some of you who will just take the women's word for it, without proof or evidence which will do a disservice to the justice system, due process and the rule of law, because you didn't care as long as the women came out on top and if a man just so happens to get caught up as collateral damage then, oh well, too bad for him.

Yeah, until it happens to one of your close male family members. Then there are those who believe that the woman is right, otherwise why would she bring a case like this up?

However, you are assuming that everyone has good morals, are honest and won't do any wrong. That's a nice way of looking at things but what if the woman has a grudge or an axe to grind with the guy? What if she's trying to extort money from him, then what? We won't know the answer to those questions because you already believed her word first and now, we have failed to follow the due process in order to find out.

Remember today's women are strong, equal, independent and very serious competitors to men in every and that includes a negative way too! Which means that women cheat just like men. Women have faults, just like men, And WOMEN LIE! JUST LIKE MEN! and that's why she would have to have some kind of proof or evidence to back up her claim and not just her word alone. We cannot as a society allow women with an agenda to weaponize sex for their own personal agenda or gain. That's them taking advantage of their being women.

What is the #MeToo Movement and what is it all about? These are women who "said" that men have sexually harassed or assaulted them in the distance past. I put "said" in quotation marks because that word is key to the #MeToo Movement since it's the only thing that backs up the women's claim that a sexual assault or harassment had even taken place.

They don't have any actual proof or evidence which is required to prove someone's guilty or innocence. In other words, all these women have is their word that a sexual assault or harassment had taken place, some ten, twenty, thirty and in some cases even forty years ago. Let that sink in for a moment.

A woman can go back forty year or more and have a man charged with sexual assault or harassment, without absolutely no proof or evidence to back up her claim. Only her word! Men are dragged into court, charged with a serious crime of sexual assault or harassment and are asked to prove that they didn't commit the crime. In other words, they are presumed guilty until proven innocent, which has turned our justice system on its head.

How can a man prove that he didn't commit the crime, in some cases from decades ago? This is a very dangerous and unfair treatment of men based only on a woman's word. Again, she has no proof or evidence that this crime actually took place at that time. Also why didn't she bring these charges up at the time that it happened? Why decades later? What's happening here is that men's rights are being taking away from them and these women are weaponizing sex.

There are some people who would say that they just believe the woman. Which means that the men are automatically guilty in their eyes based on no proof, facts or evidence. How can we as a society go forward with this kind of injustice for men by women who are weaponizing sex? These women have waged a full out assault upon men. How do we know if the men committed the crime or not? The women have no proof or evidence.

Some of you who agree with this premise maybe saying to yourself, but why would a woman make up these stories of sexual assault or harassment from decades ago if it didn't actually happen? What's her motive? That's exactly my point.

Motive? We don't know her motive, because first of all we don't know her.

Secondly, we don't know her motive because we don't have any proof or evidence from her in order to prove her case. Let me ask you this question? Is there a chance that her motive could be money or revenge? I'm sure the answer is yes there could be a chance that it's money or revenge. If that's the case that money or revenge is a possible motive that we can't take off the table, then shouldn't we as a society demand that she show some kind of proof or evidence that this crime was actually committed? And if not, why not?

We should just take her word for it and just believe her, even though money or revenge could be her motive, because we don't know her motive. That would be weaponizing sex. These women in the #MeToo Movement have weaponized sex against men because they are making men guilty of a crime that the men can't prove, totally based on what they "said" a man did to them.

These women are trying to get men put in jail based on no proof or evidence. That's a world that we can't live in today. This is a very dangerous precedent that the #MeToo Movement is setting. For those who agree with this premise had better hope that they don't have any sons, fathers, brothers, uncles or anyone in their family who is a male, because they are just maybe the next target of the #MeToo Movement. Then how would you feel about the #MeToo Movement then? I'm sure you would want your male family members to have their due process.

Right? Men and our society can't allow women to

weaponize sex and use it without due process and have men put in jail just based on some woman's word alone. What if this woman has a grudge or vendetta against the man that she is accusing? Do we still just take her word for it?

What if a woman is upset that her ex-boyfriend dumped her twenty years ago and she had to go through therapy to get over it and now she wants revenge? Do we still just take her word for it? What if a woman didn't get the promotion at work and has it out for her male boss because he was an asshole to her? Do we still just take her word for it?

What if a teacher or professor gave a woman a failing grade on a test and she failed that course and it cost her thousands of dollars and time wasted and she's upset with him because of it still? Do we still just take her word for it?

What if a man left a woman at the altar and cheated on her with her best friend, do we still just take her word for it? This is why we have the policy of assuming innocence until proven guilty and not guilty until proven innocent. This is why we have due process.

The burden of proof is on the accuser not the accused, because she brought this case to the forefront, shined the light on it and ask us to believe her, therefore a woman has to prove that a man committed this crime with actually proof and evidence. The #MeToo Movement doesn't believe in innocence until proven guilty or in due processes.

They just want you to take a woman's word for it. Even though they have no idea what the woman's motive could be in bringing these charges against a man. What if the woman just hated men? Do we still just take her word for it? I'm not saying that men didn't commit the crime in every instance.

What I'm saying is that we don't know who is telling the truth from decades ago, without any proof, facts or evidence to back it up. So, don't just put a man in jail with no proof, facts or evidence. That would be a railroad job that we in this country just can't allow. The entire #MeToo Movement is the very definition of weaponizing sex. It has gone, unchecked, unchallenged, unhinged for too long, and it's become unbalanced.

It's also the very definition of "taking advantage of being a woman." Why? These women are saying that they are victims of sexual assault or harassment, without the proof or evidence and they just want us to take their word for it solely because they are women and want us to be sympathetic to them, because they are women. That's them taking advantage of their being a woman. It's all of the above wrapped up into one movement.

Why? Because they want no due process, no fairness and no justice. Just punishment for men. That's weaponizing sex. According to women—Men, there is a price to pay for not standing up and fighting for your rights.

What do Harvey Weinstein, Bill Cosby, Justice Kavanaugh, Cuba Gooding, Jr. and many more, all have in common? They all have been targeted by the #MeToo Movement.

Harvey Weinstein was one of the most powerful entertainment moguls in the Hollywood. He was not confronted or charged with any specific evidence or proof of a crime. He was charged based upon his reputation. Every knows that Hollywood is a cesspool for lust. It's part of the culture and everyone turned a blind eye to that behavior, including powerful women like Hillary Clinton and Oprah Winfrey because they wanted the financial and political backing from Harvey Weinstein.

Hollywood eats, sleeps and breeds sex, which is a recipe for disaster. Everyone in Hollywood knows about the "casting couch". The "casting couch" is when someone like a director or producer withholds a part in a movie or recorded deal or something of value from the actors or musicians, until they have sex with them, and if they don't, then they don't get the part.

Basically, it is sexual exploitation, and extortion. The reason it's not rape or sexual assault is because the person volunteered and it wasn't forced sexual assault. The actors or musicians could have very easily walked away from the slimy creep who makes the conditions, but they wanted the part and so they go along with it. Having consensual sex is not a crime. The "casting couch" maybe sleazy but it is not a crime.

However, the #MeToo Movement targeted Weinstein and an actress charged him with rape, without proof, just only her word. I'm not making any excuses for or siding with Harvey Weinstein, because he probably did commit the crime; however even this creepy slimeball still has a right to due process. We don't want to convict a person based solely on his reputation; we want to convict him based on the evidence.

A good reason why is because we don't want to encourage copycat incidents or opportunistic women making false claims in order to get a larger paycheck because she knows that everyone would believe her lie based on a defendant's bad reputation. In the case of Bill Cosby more than fifty women came out and they all had the same or similar story.

They all said that he drugged and raped them. However not one of them reported the sexual assault to the police. That's amazing. You may ask why is that amazing? It amazing because I find it hard to believe it when they said that they can remember with vivid details the drugs and sexual assault today, which is almost thirty or forty years ago, but they couldn't remember them when it was closer to the date that it happened.

Memories fade over time, and they don't improve with time. Also, every one of them had the same alibi too, which is that they didn't report before because they thought no one would have believed them. That's very interesting. Why? This has to be the biggest coincidence or it's a lie.

Why? Because it sounds like they couldn't come up with a good answer to justify why they didn't tell someone or call the police, so that when they heard one woman say it so they all said it because then they can justify the reason they want to charge him now but not then.

It is something that has to fit the narrative. However, I do understand that they wouldn't be able to remember the assault because they may had been drugged. But if you don't remember the assault because you were drugged and unconscious, how do you know it actually took place? Because they said that they were unconscious.

That makes no sense to me. Now, an incredible amount of time has gone by, in some case decades, and these women's memories are as sharp and vivid as ever? Now all of a sudden once they hear about a woman who claims she got assault by Bill Cosby and got paid, and then this somehow triggered their memory because of the other women coming forward, right?

That sounds like either the strangest coincidence or are everyone or some of these women are lying? I say that because of the fact that no one, NOT one woman reported the assault to the authorities at that time. How can every woman have the same story of rape and also the same identical story of why they didn't report it?

The stories sound kind of funny. It kind of sounds like a lie. I don't know if any of what they said happened or not, and neither do you because none of us were there. This is why we need proof and evidence so that we can sort out the facts from the fiction. Then we can make a reasonable judgment. That's how it works. Also, we still need due process. Because these women could be telling the truth, or they could be lying. Only the facts, evidence and proof can solve the mystery.

With Justice Kavanaugh, we all saw that circus show and it was a terrible disaster. The political hacks were out for blood. They pushed that woman up there and used her to try and bring that man down and their agenda was clear. The #MeToo Movement showed their true colors. This was not about a sexual assault from almost forty years ago. This was about weaponizing sex.

This was an attempt in using a sexual assault claim to destroy a potentially Supreme Court Justice, in order to keep Roe v. Wade alive. This is why we need due process. This is why we need facts, evidence and proof that a crime has actually been committed, because Dr. Ford's motive for bringing this case to Congress was the political agenda of someone else, and not hers. Therefore #MeToo Movement cannot go unchecked, unchallenged, unhinged because it is unbalanced.

Cuba Gooding, Jr. was at a club or bar and a random, uninvited woman walked up to him and his girlfriend and injected herself into the conversation. It appeared as if she was introducing herself and her hand was close to her chest while she was holding a drink. Cuba then touched her leg as if he was speaking to her, then he grabbed her hand which was still close to her chest and the he pulled her hand towards him and kissed the woman's hand as if he was greeting her or thanking her.

Then out of nowhere some guy came up to the woman and proceeded to bump and grind on the woman in a sexual way. Now Cuba's girlfriend was in between him and the woman the entire time. He literally had reach over his girlfriend in order to grab the woman's hand. At no time was the woman and Cuba alone. Cuba then got up and left the room and the woman followed them almost everywhere they went.

It was like she was stalking him. I remember this was eight years ago. Ever since the year of 2018 and the #MeToo movement was born, women have been bringing up old outdated clams with absolutely no proof or evidence to back up their claim. Now this woman who accused Cuba thought she had a video tape to back her claim up, but the video shows a general casual meeting with the star Cuba Gooding, Jr.

Now remember the unknown random guy who actually grinds on her? He was never charged or even brought up. I guess he had no money. So, if she was so hurt and offended by sexual misconduct then why didn't she charge the other guy with sexual assault? This is clearly a woman who is trying to capitalize on the #MeToo Movement and get her fifteen minutes of fame.

She was weaponizing sex against Cuba but not the other guy who was actually offensive towards her. This woman needs to be held accountable for this BS claim that she has brought to the justice system when there are real and serious sexual assaults that the police could be pursuing with the resources that was now being tied up because of an opportunistic woman. This is what taking advantage of being a woman is.

Still don't believe it's about a power grab? Ok, well strap on your seat belts and let's take a ride down reality lane, because here comes your proof!

A woman name E. Jean Carroll accused President Trump of sexual assault. This was in June of 2019. I was watching CNN as the anchor Alisyn Camerota was trying to get this woman to file a police report against her will, and the CNN anchor was asking leading questions like "do you want to file a case", "you know the statute of limitations law was changed so you can still file if you want too", "the mayor of New York City, who is running for president in 2020 by the way, will take up your case and investigate it for you against President Trump if you file".

I mean, this CNN anchor Alisyn was really egging this woman on, but it was obvious that the woman didn't want to do it only so that the New York City mayor Bill de Blasio can use it against President Trump in the 2020 campaign, so that he and the Democrats can use that inflammatory information to get women upset at President Trump so that they will vote against him to the point where he will lose his 2020 re-election bid.

Clearly that's weaponizing Sex. Now take it, this woman, E. Jean Carroll had just written a book entitled *What Do We Need Men For?* and was promoting that book on CNN. And she made the comment that it is women's turn to be in power because the men have had their turn. It's clearly a political power grab that the #MeToo Movement is all about and pushing. This woman was even reluctant to say that she was raped or abused by President Trump.

She was more concerned about how women can use these old sexual assault claims to further the women cause to take overpower from men. Immediately after the Ms. Carroll segment was over, CNN did a different segment on the same topic with a three women panel, who all don't like the president, including one of their own reporters, on how to use this woman's sexual assault allegations against President Trump.

They were planning and plotting on how to divide the Republican Party by asking the senators and members of congress why they would stand by the president after this woman had accused him of this alleged crime. They were plotting and planning on how to shame the Republican members in order to put pressure on them to divide and to break away from their support of the president.

These women also were planning and plotting on how to rile up women voters, get them mad and upset at the president so that they would not support him in the 2020 election. Now, remember this woman, Ms. Carroll has no proof, no evidence, and no facts to back up her allegations. So how do we know what she alleged is true or not? I guess we just have to take her word for it right?

And are those the same words that went into her man hating book that she is promoting, entitled, *What Do We Need Men For?* But that didn't stop CNN from pushing this story and trying to find a way to weaponize the sexual assault claim and attempt to bring down President Trump with unverified allegations. I watched CNN the next day and they did another segment on Ms. Carroll's story about the President.

I watched as the CNN anchors, pundits and guess were so upset and disappointed that the story wasn't going to grow and have the legs needed in order to bring President Trump down. They weren't talking about Ms. Carroll sexual assault claim and how it affected her life. They were talking about how to politicize it and use this #MeToo moment to pile allegations upon the President, hoping that this would anger women to the point where it will hurt his chances with women voters so that they can get him out of office.

Now what part of this is about justice for the so-called sexual assault "victim"? They are plotting a presidential change of power. Which means that's this is about a power grab. So, there is clearly an agenda from the #MeToo Movement, which is fueled by the media in order to take down a president by weaponizing sex.

After all of that political talk about President Trump and using sexual assault allegations against him, I was wondering how this was about a woman and how she was assaulted? I guess it was not about that! CNN and the mainstream news media are more concerned about how to use the sexual allegations against the President as a political tool in order bring down the most powerful man on earth, than they are about the so-called "victim." Hmmm, I wonder why that is?

Sounds a lot like weaponizing sex to me. But I guess I'm just delusional. Who am I supposed to believe, the #MeToo Movement, or my lying eyes and my lying ears? This is clearly weaponizing sex and a power grab and not about justice for sexual assault to use allegations to try to influence the presidential election of 2020. Check and mate!

Case closed!

CHAPTER 4

THE PAY GAP HOAX

Equal Pay for Equal work?
or is it a Con Game in Order to Gain Sympathy and an
Advantage Over Men?

IF WOMEN WERE STILL VICTIMS OF MALE OPPRESSION AND SUPPRESSION THEN WHY DO WOMEN OUTNUMBER MEN in colleges and universities, the workplace, and have made tremendous accomplishments that are equal or better than men? The PAY GAP is a complete HOAX on a global scale.

Why? BECAUSE FEMINISTS AND WOMEN'S GROUPS ARE INTENTIONALLY HIDING THE TRUE FACTS AND ARE NOT ACCURATELY EXPLAINING ALL OF THE VARIABLES INVOLVED AS TO HOW THEY CAME UP WITH PAY GAP NUMBERS OF UNEQUAL PAY BETWEEN MEN AND WOMEN!

Here's what I mean. By women maintaining their so-called 'VICTIM STATUS' they can continuously receive sympathy, preferential treatment, special privileges, and favorable advantages over men for being treated so-called "unfairly" that way they can get political funding, economic power, and get other women to join together, because there's strength in numbers.

They can be sexist towards men (and get away with it), silence and censor men's voices and opinions with NO checks or challenges and that way men can't oppose them in anyway otherwise they will smear them claiming 'VICTIM STATUS' and that men are 'OFFENSIVELY' attacking women.

That's why women stay under the radar and undetected as they plan and plot their HOSTILE TAKE OVER BY SILENCING AND CENSORING MEN, SO THAT MEN CAN'T FIGHT WOMEN BACK OR COMPETE BACK WITH WOMEN, THEREFORE GIVING WOMEN A FREE PASS, UNOPPOSED, UNCHALLENGED AND AN UNCHECKED RIDE INTO POWER AND CONTROL TO CONQUER WITH THEIR AGENDA WHICH IS WORLD DOMINANCE OVER MEN!

Also, women are 'continuously' claiming to be victims of "OFFENSIVE" language and SEXIST ATTACKS by men on everything that they dislike, disagree with or doesn't favor them. This is a way that women get to silence and censor men's voices at will in any given situation with no opposition, with these MANUFACTURED OUTRAGE TACTICS.

This is how women usually gain advantage, control, and power over men. By the time men figure out that this is a WAR UPON THEM AND A HOSTILE TAKE DOWN, it will be too late and women would have already taken power and control both politically and economically over them by their TAKING ADVANTAGE OF BEING WOMEN!

By getting women to continuously play the part of the victim (and at the same time claiming to be strong, independent, and equal) feminists and women's groups get men to help them gain these advantages, to take control and power over the very men who are helping them.

This is a slick and deceptive way of their taking advantage of being women (by having it both ways) and using men to WORK AGAINST OTHER MEN AND THEIR OWN BEST INTERESTS IN ORDER TO FAVOR WOMEN OVER MEN.

IT'S CALLED, DIVIDE AND CONQUER!

This is the reason why you hear women suggest to men to HELP WOMEN COME UP FROM A DEPRESSING SITUATION! AS IF THEY ARE 'STILL' VICTIMS' OF MALE OPPRESSION AND SUPPRESSION, FOR IN REALITY, WOMEN HAVE ALREADY SURPASSED MEN IN ALMOST EVERY CATEGORY BOTH ECONOMICAL AND POLITICAL.

THE DECEITFUL PLOT IS TO GET MEN TO HELP WOMEN DEFEAT MEN!

I HAVE A QUESTION FOR MEN AND THE READERS OF THIS BOOK. IN TODAY'S SOCIETY HERE IN AMERICA, WHERE HAVE SEEN (ON A MASS SCALE), AND IN WHAT CATEGORY OR AREA, WOMEN "STILL" BEING OPPRESSED BY MEN? NOT IN THE PAST, NOT WHAT YOU'VE BEEN TOLD OR HEARD BY FEMINIST OR OTHERS, BUT WHAT YOU YOURSELF HAVE WITNESSED WITH YOUR OWN TWO EYES? SHOW ME THE PROOF! I'M QUITE SURE THE ANSWER IS —NONE!

You haven't seen it. Otherwise it would be front page breaking news on every broadcast and cable news outlet.

Because that would be considered blatant discrimination in the workplace against women. But yet—every woman in the country is saying and repeating the feminist talking point that there is a PAY GAP between men and women but provide NO specific company's name or individual person or victims who can come forward to back up their claims. Why is that? I'll tell you why. It's because it doesn't exist!

IT'S A HOAX AND A FRAUD ON MEN CREATED IN ORDER GAIN SYMPATHY FOR WOMEN BEING A SO-CALLED "VICTIM OF MALE SUPPRESSION AND OPPRESSION" (WHICH IS NOT TRUE), IN ORDER TO GET OTHER MEN TO HELP WOMEN TO DESTROY MALE POWER AND TO DEFEAT MEN SO THAT WOMEN CAN SEIZE AND TAKE AWAY THAT SAME POWER FOR THEMSELVES. THE PAY GAP (IN TODAY'S SOCIETY, NOT THE PAST) IS THE BIGGEST HOAX AND CON JOB IN THE WORLD!

If you don't believe it, men—challenge any woman to show you proof that the pay gap "STILL" exists in today's society (NOT IN THE PAST) with a man's and woman's pay stub who do the same job, with a similar spent time frame on the job, (i.e. not a man whose been on the job for ten years with pay raise increases for good performance versus a woman fresh out of college with no pay raise for her spent time) and from the same company and my guess is that— SHE CANNOT SHOW YOU THIS "MONEY GAP!"

IN A WORLD WHERE ALMOST EVERY WOMAN SAYS OR CLAIMS THAT SHE IS STRONG, INDEPENDENT AND EQUAL TO MEN IN EVERY WAY, WHY DO MOST WOMEN STILL CLAIM TO BE VICTIMS OF MALE OPPRESSION? THIS IS BECAUSE CLAIMING SO-CALLED "VICTIM STATUS" HAS GREAT BENEFITS TO WOMEN. THE REASON THEY WANT TO HOLD ON

TO THEIR SO-CALLED "VICTIM STATUS" BECAUSE IT GIVES THEM GREAT COMFORT. IT'S LIKE AN INSURANCE POLICY TO CONTROL MEN AND GAIN AN ADVANTAGE OVER THEM.

Women use the so-called "victim status" to keep men in check. The reason is that women get a strategic advantage over men by playing the victim. Women get preferential treatment for being a victim. Women get special privileges for playing the victim. Women get favorable advantages for being seen as the victim.

These are the reasons why women continuously SAY that they are "OFFENDED" by men. Because when women say that things are "OFFENSIVE" to them, it automatically makes them a "VICTIM" and now they can then control men by SILENCING AND CENSORING their behavior or language. It's the ultimate control SWITCH to shut men up and shut them down, and that gives women free passes to BULLY MEN and make them bow down to them so they can take power and control away from them and gain it for themselves. It's their TAKING ADVANTAGE OF BEING WOMEN.

By having it both ways women take all the advantages and men must do whatever they say they want otherwise men will get smeared for committing an OFFENSIVE, SEXIST ATTACK ON WOMEN. This is a slick, deceitful con game played by women and it just needs to be EXPOSED! This is why they SAY they are victims of sexism by men. Therefore, they continuously play the gender card when things don't go their way.

WHEN WOMEN PLAY THE VICTIM, IT IS ONE BIG HOAX AND CON JOB BY WOMEN IN ORDER TO FLY UNDER THE RADAR UNDETECTED SO THAT MEN WON'T BE AWARE OF THEIR FRAUDULENT CON GAME THAT THEY PERPETRATE ON THEM. AND

THAT'S TO GET MEN TO HELP THEM TAKE AWAY POWER AND CONTROL FROM OTHER MEN (AND FROM THE VERY MEN WHO ARE HELPING THEM) AND GAIN IT FOR THEMSELVES. A SLICK UNDERHANDED HOSTILE TAKE DOWN OF MEN!

THIS IS WHY YOU HEAR THE PHRASE—#I'M WITH HER! It is a ploy in order to get you as a man to go along with the "VICTIM STATUS" scam and con game! And at the same time these women are trying to get you as a man to help YOU destroy yourself.

CHAPTER 5

UNCHECKED-
UNCHALLENGED
UNHINGED &
UNBALANCED

Women crossing the line into men's rights—While at the same time Making it Offensive and Sexist to Compete with— Challenge or Oppose Them!

In this world that we live in today everything and everyone has checks and balances. Why? Because checks and balances keep everyone and everything fair, honest and equal. We, as a society, need this fairness in our lives in order to make sure that one thing doesn't dominate another which causes the weaker ones to go extinct. Every mouse has its cat and every cat has its dog. Lions have their hyenas and hyenas has their lions. The President has Congress and Congress has the Senate and the Senate has the President, and vice versa, which makes things balanced because each one checks the other out.

That makes things fair so that no one dominates the other to the point where it causes their extinction. Now we come to male and female, women and men. In our society men have dominated the workplace and the political arena and the home for centuries. Now in today's world the women's empowerment movement has come up to the point where it has checked and balanced out a lot of the unfairness that men have caused and have benefited from.

Women in mass numbers have entered and enrolled in colleges, universities and the workplace to the point where they are now the majority. Now that women have put a check on men, men can no longer abuse women without there being consequences for their action. Women's salaries have come up to the point where some women are making more money than men.

I know some of you may think that it's still not where it should be yet, and that's a fair statement. However, research hasn't shown the exact calculated numbers so this can be debated. Women have made tremendous progress in the workplace and with their pay. Now, in today's society women have begun to make their own rules. They've made it so that men can't offend women otherwise they will be publicly shamed, lose their jobs or be put in jail.

Therefore, there should be consequences and repercussions for their negative actions. With all the progress that women have accomplished and achieved through the last couple of decades, they have gone unchecked and unchallenged because they have made men afraid of them due to backlash. As soon as a man challenges or tries to check a woman for her bad or negative behavior, she tries to intimidate and bully him.

Women try to shut men up and shut them down by making them out to be sexists, offensive for attacking women. Therefore, they go unchecked, unchallenged and unbalanced. So if everyone and everything has checks and balances, and women have come up to keep men in check from dominating everything, then who's putting a check on the women to make sure that they haven't gone too far the other way to the point where now they are unfairly dominating men?

Which is what we have today in our system. The answer to this question over the last couple decades and to the present day is—NO ONE—because women have gone unchecked and unchallenged and now there is no balance for the men anymore. A man can't tell a woman what to do or give his opinion or advice without women viewing it as offensive or as an attack upon women.

Which means she proceeds unchecked and unchallenged. In today's society women have become more aggressive in getting their way, and now many of them have become bullies to men, because women have made it get to the point where men can't fight back or challenge them in any kind of way, and that includes physical (even when a man is defending himself) because that would be considered abuse, disrespectful and offensive and an attack on women.

Therefore, if women have made it so that they can't be checked or challenged, because they view it as an offensive attack on women, then where is the balance? There is none and that's the problem with today's men and women relationships in the home and at the workplace. Women have made the claim that they are strong independent and equal to men in every way.

They have come up financially to balance the power of men. They have their own houses, cars and personal possessions. They don't need a man to take care of them anymore, because they can do that for themselves. So, if all of this is true and they have all of this progress, accomplishments and achievements, and they are a serious competitor to men in every way, then why is there still no balance? Why are we continuously treating women as if they are weaker? Why are we treating women with so-called kid gloves when they do something wrong and it's time for them to be held accountable for their actions?

In other words, the balance of negative dominance has flipped from men to women. At a point in the past men's negative actions had gone too far and women needed to put a check on the negative control that men once had. Now women have the negative dominating power and control because they've made it so that men can't check or challenge them in anyway, without it considered being offensive or an attack on all women, therefore things have become unbalanced.

Things have gone from too far in favor of men in the past, to having gone too far in favor of women today. How so? Because now women can check and challenge men, but men can't check and challenge women and that's where the problem lies. Therefore, men must now challenge women regardless of the backlash in order to keep things fair, honest and balanced, which is what we all want. Equality, right?

CHAPTER 6

THE PLOT TO SEEK AND DESTROY ALL THINGS MALE

Male Suppression

THE AGENDA MAKING
MEN OBSOLETE

If women are allowed to smear, vilify, tear down and damage the male gender as a whole, then they can take down every man in power and replace them with women-- which gives women TOTAL DOMINANCE over men and sole power and control-- Which means-- NO BALANCE- NO FAIRNESS & NO DUE PROCESS FOR MEN,
AKA
#METOO!

Therefore Creating
A POWER GRAB
By GENDER ASSASSINATION

Why are feminist women trying to seek and destroy all things male? It's because that's the only way they can gain power and control over men. Which is their agenda. To take away power and control from men and gain it for themselves. However, they don't want an even or equal or a fair fight, because it may not accomplish their goal. Therefore, the feminists are going through the back door or around the rules.

Rather than to keep trying to break the glass ceiling with no success, they are trying to smear and tear the male gender as a whole so that men are depicted as "damaged goods" to make it easier for them to make their case that men shouldn't be trusted with power therefore we have to replace them with women.

Don't believe it? Then why are all the 2020 female Democratic presidential candidates saying things like we need a woman in the White House. They are not asking the best person for the job be placed there, they only want a woman regardless of her qualifications.

However, the implication is clear that NO MALE NEED APPLY! Therefore, this shows what lengths women would go to destroy any man or males that would challenge or threaten their agenda. This does not just apply to the presidency. This feminist agenda has been employed throughout the media, Television, movies, the entertainment industry's, corporate workplace and anywhere women can gain power over men.

Men have been asleep at the wheel while this agenda has been employed between the cracks and through the back door! Women's agenda to destroy all things male is their gateway to permanent power, which will have men intimidated and catering to women's need as their servants.

Men—you must MAN UP and challenge this HOSTILE TAKE DOWN. Otherwise you will be continuously treated unfairly with NO DUE PROCESS! You must adopt the attitude of—-"FRANKLY MY DEAR I DON'T GIVE A DAMN."

This is for your own survival! Because your rights to exist as MAN is in serious and imminent danger! If you don't believe me just take a look around you. You have to check and double check your language every time you are around a woman in order to make sure that you don't offend her as if she is above you like a princess sitting on the throne who can do NO wrong—am I Right? I know I am.

This should wake up every man—that your rights to equality and free speech has been taking from you without your knowledge or permission! YOUR EQUALITY AND FREEDOM OF SPEACH HAS BEEN DESTROYED—MAKING MEN OBSOLETE!

What is male suppression? Male suppression is when women or powerful entities like the media try to omit or downplay any and all things male and men's accomplishments which make men look better and/or stronger than women, even in the cases that it is true. If a woman can't measure up to a man in certain areas or situations, like physical strength or sports then women, or the media, will try to find some other areas where the men look weak, failed or didn't accomplish something in order to take the focus off of the women's short comings or failures.

Then they highlight men's failures that are unrelated to make women feel comfortable that they are not failing alone and view women in a positive light and at the same time make men look incompetent. If you watch television, then you will see this in depth. In sitcoms, television commercials, and movies you will see that the men are the butt of every joke and are made to look like bumbling fools.

You will also see that it is the women that have to teach the man about a specific product as if the man is just some kind of dumb idiot with two left feet, and basically a clown or a buffoon. You will also see that the men have to get a helping hand or some kind of assistance from a woman and not to the other way around.

You will see almost constantly that the women are the heroes and have to save the man. She is strong and he is weak. He cooks and cleans for her, while she works outside the home, A.K.A. the bread winner. He lives with her in her house. She never lives with him in his house. All of this is so that the man looks weak and the woman looks strong. Reversing the roles so that the women look and feel empowered and at the same time the men's accomplishments are intentionally omitted or suppressed and they are made to appear as weak.

Today's society doesn't want a man to look or appear to be strong because it makes a woman look weak and that's what society is trying to avoid. That's the narrative the media and many women's groups want to project.

Why do women and society want to suppress and destroy

men's accomplishments? Because there is an agenda by women's groups to take over political and economic power and be the voice of this generation. Believe it or not. If you don't believe it? Then explain why the Democrat party is pushing a woman candidate for the 2020 presidential election with the mainstream media backing them up and at the same time suppressing men by saying things like white males have destroyed this country and shouldn't be trusted anymore.

Explain why are democratic women are against their own party's male candidate and saying things like "we don't want another white male", "it's time for a female president", even though the men are leading in all the 2020 polls? Explain why when women achieve something like in sports, it's used against men, and to put them down?

Example: The 2019 U.S women soccer team scored a total of sixteen goals in two games. Nice, congratulations so far. Right? However, it was used in the sports media to put the men's team down. Sports commentators said things like, "yeah, the women scored sixteen goals in two games, but the men's team only scored twelve goals in the entire tournament." What did the men's teams' accomplishments have to do with the women's accomplishments?

Absolutely nothing. It was used to belittle men and to tear them down. What if we belittled women in the same way? I'm quite sure it would be called sexist and there would be an outrage by women's groups and the media. There are plenty of sports where men have great accomplishments over women, but you don't hear about them because the media and women's groups don't want to emphasize men's triumphs over women.

So those accomplishments are not talked about or discussed, and they are intentionally suppressed by the media because they want to have a woman president and women in power. Men have achieved great things in this world. Hell, men literally built this world! It's sad that we have to suppress men's accomplishments because women's egos can't take a man doing anything better than them. I say too damn bad!

Men should stand up and be enormously proud of their accomplishments and achievements, just like women are empowered by their accomplishments. After all, men have work so hard to achieve these things and shouldn't have to suppress them just to appease a woman's ego. Men—be proud of what you have accomplished and own it. Don't let nobody step on your glory because they are jealous or hating on you.

After all these same women will not let you step on their accomplishments because they see that as sexist. They will call you sexist and every other name in the book if they can. They would never try to appease a man's ego. So why should a man appease *their* ego? Everyone should be proud of their hard-earned achievements and nobody should be trying to tear the other gender down just because they are driven by power.

Therefore, men, don't try to appease them. Don't let anyone suppress you. So, if women or the media try to make fools of you (men), stand up for yourself. Don't buy products that denigrate you. After all that's why companies don't denigrate women in their advertising, because they know if they offend women, then women's groups will boycott their products. So, what's good for the goose should be good for the gander.

In today's society a man can't be proud of his accomplishments or have any public glory because he has to worry about appeasing women or else the women's groups will try to tear them down by labeling them as bolstering, bragging, cocky and sexist (playing the gender card). A man shouldn't have to suppress his true feelings or not let it out that he feels good about himself and his accomplishments just because a woman's pride or feelings might get hurt.

Unlike women, who bolster and brag every chance they get when they have achieved something, especially when a woman achieves it over a man. This double standard has driven some men to the point where they just don't give a damn how a woman feels anymore. They are tired of being suppressed which makes them depressed, even though they should be happy and feel good about what they have achieved and accomplished. If we are as equal as women say that we are, then women have to check their egos at the door and accept men's achievements positively just like men should accept theirs.

However, this will not happen because women and the women's groups have a hidden agenda to take over political and economic power, and this is what's driving the push for MALE SUPPRESSION. For those who don't believe that there is a movement to seek and destroy all things male in this country—let me direct your focus to Berkeley, California where they are changing and taking down the names of all things men.

Example. The city of Berkeley has changed the name of "manhole" and "manpower" to "maintenance hole" and "work force". These changes were made in order to destroy any thing that makes men look superior over women. This agenda is to take out and suppress men's accomplishments so that it can be gender neutral therefore women can replace it or fill the slot of the men, also known as a power change or flipping the balance of power from men to women.

Some of you may say "well, what's wrong with women being in power or control?" I say that there is nothing wrong with women being in power. However, if they are going to seek and destroy all things male and suppress men in order to gain that power then everything is wrong with it. Men shouldn't be suppressed or stifled by women just so that they can take power away from men. This is UNAMERICAN and should not be tolerated by men.

However, if women actually earn that power then that's okay and good for the country, BUT if women want to seize power through male suppression, weaponizing gender, and taking advantage of their being a woman, then there is going to be a fight and a gender war. Men will no longer stand by while some women's groups assassinate their characters through gender.

Men will have to hold women accountable for their actions and not treat them with kid gloves anymore when they say that they are strong independent women who are equal to men in every way. Women can no longer get free passes just for being a woman, when they are SERIOUS COMPETITORS to men in the workplace and in the home. Women are competing with men for the same jobs, same political positions, and economic issues and therefore women have to be treated as a truly equal power, which means that they can no longer get respect for just being a woman; they have to earn it just like men.

They can no longer claim victim status for being the weaker gender as a woman, when they are equal to men. They can no longer get emotional breaks for being a woman when they are supposed to be serious competitors to men. Otherwise this means that they would be taking advantage of their being a woman and NOT truly equal to men.

Women can no longer say to men, "why are you disrespectful to women" as if they are special and above men to be treated like princesses. Women can no longer say to men, "you shouldn't treat a woman that way", as if she is precious, privileged and entitled just for her gender.

Women can no longer be give preferential treatment, as "women or ladies first", since they are equal to men in every way, otherwise they would be taking advantage of their being women and runs counter to their notions of equality despite their claims.

Why do women believe that they should come before men, when they themselves say that are equal in every way? The "ladies first" concept is NOT giving them the equality they claim to have. Today's women can no longer use emotions, their sensitivity, or portrayal as a victim in order to get favorable treatment because they are supposed to be very serious competitors to men.

Today's women must be held accountable for their actions when they are wrong and can no longer be treated with kid gloves; meaning that we treat them like a child who can't handle the truth.

And to all of those who don't like it or disagree with it —
I say unto you—

"FRANKLY MY DEAR I DON'T GIVE A DAMN!"

ENOUGH IS ENOUGH!

Men have a First Amendment right to voice their opinions
and defend themselves just like strong independent women.
There is nothing wrong with that—It's a good thing for women!

BUT MEN WILL NO LONGER BOW DOWN, GIVE
IN & GIVE A FREE PASS TO STRONG, -EQUAL- AND
INDEPENDENT WOMEN, WHO ARE VERY SERIOUS
COMPETITORS TO MEN!
THEY MUST STAND ON THEIR OWN TWO FEET
AND HOLD THEIR OWN (JUST LIKE A MAN)
AND BE TRULY EQUAL (JUST LIKE THEY CLAIM
THEY ARE) & THAT MEANS THAT THEY HAVE TO
TAKE THE GOOD WITH THE BAD & THE POSITIVE
WITH THE NEGATIVE!
BECAUSE MEN WILL COMPETE BACK!
—BECAUSE—
MEN COMPETING BACK IS NOT AN ATTACK ON
WOMEN!
MEN DEFENDING THEMSELVES IS NOT
OFFENSIVE &
MEN VOICING THEIR OPINIONS AND SPEAKING
THEIR MINDS —IS NOT SEXIST— IT IS THEIR FIRST

AMENDMENT AMERICAN RIGHT!

And to all those who don't like it or who disagree with it I say unto you—

"FRANKLY MY DEAR I DON'T GIVE A DAMN"

MEN, YOUR EXISTENCE AS A MAN IS UNDER ATTACK AND IS IN SERIOUS AND IMMINENT DANGER!

MAN UP!

There's a target on your back!
& A PRICE TO PAY!
ARE YOU PREPARED TO PAY IT?
You have NO IDEA how much you don't know!

CHAPTER 7

THERE'S A PRICE TO PAY

If You Don't Man up!

Most women make a man pay some kind of a price for having sex with them. That price could be money, gifts, entertainment, household chores, like taking out the trash or washing dishes, handy work, walking in the park a picnic on the beach, dinner and a movie, cuddling on the sofa watching television, and so on.

It doesn't matter the women's interests, the point is that there's a price for men to pay, and women are the sexual gatekeepers and they are in charge of all sex activities with the exception of any forced assault. Therefore, most women (not all there are exceptions) have weaponized sex for their own personal gain. Many women will require something from a man in exchange for him to have sex with her.

Women make men pay them a price to have sex with them

because they can. It's because they know that they are the sexual gatekeepers and therefore men would have to comply with their rules for having sexual relations with them. Don't believe it? Then men, ask any woman to have sex with you and see what she says. I guarantee you that she will want something first, before she agrees to have sex with you.

She will make a man set up a dinner date or a movie or something along those lines before she consents to having sex. You may say, "well what's wrong with that?" Nothing, if you're a woman because you would be getting a two for one deal. A woman would get gifts plus sex out of the situation. However, if you are a man then there's a lot that's wrong with it.

Most women will use sex as a bargaining tool or a weapon against men. Why? Because a woman knows that a man would be willing to do whatever it takes to have sex with an attractive woman in order to satisfy his need for sex. However, most men try to beat women to the punch by telling her what she wants to hear. What do I mean by that?

A man will come home with flowers and candy in order to sweeten a woman up first before he asks her for sex because he knows that she is going to ask for something in exchange for sex. A man will ask a woman out on a date first, with the intention of asking her for sex later. A man will take a woman on a trip or buy her jewelry or a car in order to have continuous sex with her.

A man does these things first in order to make it appear as if he is thoughtful but in reality, he does them because he knows he has to pay a price to have sex with her. Therefore, he tries to beat her at her own game. There are not many women who would trade a man straight up sex for sex. Why not? Because women know that they are the sexual gatekeepers and men have to pay their dues to her.

Some women have even taken it from favor to weaponizing. What do I mean? Some women have had sex with men, clearly consenting then turn around and threaten them with an accusation of sexual assault, rape or a lawsuit in order to get a monetary gain out of the situation. Many times, this is done against a man with great wealth or a famous person and celebrity that is the target of these women's gain.

Take the case of Kobe Bryant ex-basketball player of the LA Lakers. A woman accused him of raping her, but Kobe said it was consensual. The woman filed charges against Kobe, and it went to trial. However, during the discovery part of the trial, it had come out that the woman had five (5) different men's DNA in her panties, the one she claimed to have had on the night in question.

When that information came out the woman quickly dropped the criminal part of the case and settled out of court for money. Now if you are a woman and some man had raped you wouldn't you want to see that man go to jail for violating you? Instead, this woman settled for money which led many people to believe that that was her goal the entire time. I'm not saying that a rape did or didn't happen, but it looks very suspicious to me.

She led us to believe that this was a vicious and violent act but yet she settled for money. I guess the money healed all of her pain and emotional scars and made everything okay for her? Even at the expense of letting her so-called attacker go. I'm (SMH) shaking my head. That was weaponizing sex right there, and a price had to be paid.

CHAPTER 8

WHY HAVE WOMEN BECOME MORE MASCULINE AND LESS FEMININE IN THEIR QUEST TO BE EQUAL TO MEN?

— I'm Just as Manly as You! —

— I'm in touch with my masculine side —

In today's society I hear women saying about other women, "she is a girly-girl". That sounds very strange to me as a man, coming from another woman. So, if she is girly, which means that she is very feminine, then what is the woman who is calling her girly? Masculine?

Many of today's women talk in a masculine way, they walk in a masculine way, dress masculine, they drink and smoke like a masculine man, and they have casual sex like a masculine man. Therefore, it follows that if it walks like a duck, and quacks like a duck, then it's a duck. If many of today's women (not all) talk like a masculine man, walk like masculine man, dress like a masculine man, eat, sleep, drink and smoke like a masculine man, then they are masculine.

In today's society most women want to be equal to men in every way. They want to compete on every level. Now, many of you may be thinking, "well what's wrong with that?" Nothing, if a woman wants to do a traditional job that's held by men or in a male dominated field then she should be allowed to do that job. However, if the job requires brute strength, toughness and being masculine to do that job, then she would have to sacrifice her femininity to do it.

Here's what I mean. The more a woman wants to be equal to a man, the more she begins to behave and act like a man, which means the more masculine she becomes, the less femininity she displays, and the less feminine she is, and the less a man is attracted to her. Because men are naturally attracted to a woman's femininity, just like a woman is attracted to a man's masculinity.

Therefore, she will no longer have the sweet, and soft-spoken manner that most men are attracted to. Why not? Because she needs prove a point to every man and everyone else, that she is equal to a man in her field or at her job or in any situation, so that they can't question her toughness or ability to do that job, or that she can keep up with the men in her field. This requires acting and behaving just like her male coworkers.

Let me give you an example of how a woman can go from feminine to masculine based on her job or career. Let's look at a woman police officer. At one time that was considered a man's job because of the tough and dangerous nature that comes with the territory and environment. Tough and rough are the men who commit crimes and the police have to apprehended them by using strength and brute force, because sometimes the criminal doesn't want to go willing and would likely put up resistance in order to not go to jail.

A woman's ability in that line of work was questioned because she was considered too soft, not strong enough, not tough enough and too feminine. By a woman being feminine, she was kept out of this field or line of work because they thought that the criminal wouldn't take her seriously and that she wouldn't be able to handle him physically.

Therefore, if a woman wanted to get into this line of work and become a police officer then something had to change in her attitude and her ability to do the job. Which means that she could no longer display her feminine side because it would be seen or viewed as a negative and as a weakness that could be exploited by a criminal.

Therefore a woman had to become more tough and rougher in her mentality, in physical regimen and daily routine so that she can prove to her employers, her male coworkers, to herself and to criminals themselves that she is very much capable of doing the job, just like a man. She had to lose and shed her feminine shell and put on that masculine "armor" every day she works and now she fuses this attitude with herself and will become that rough and tough person that she changes herself to be and becomes—masculine.

Women like this police officer and other women in a male dominated workplace, which women have entered and broken the glass ceiling of, have become more masculine and less feminine and the proof is in their attitude and behavior. Here's what I mean; go and talk to a female police officer and see how she will address and talk to you. I guarantee you that she's going to talk like she's tough.

Why? Because she can't show anybody her weaknesses like she perceives her femininity to be. Talk to any woman who is in the workplace with men today and watch how they carry themselves. From their handshakes to the tones of their voices, you will find they will put more bass in their voices to sound more authoritative, masculine and in control. These women have become more masculine because of the jobs or careers, because they believe that that's the only way that they can be taken seriously on the job.

I remember back in the eighties and nineties women use to dress in suits and cut their hair short or very low in order to look like or imitate a man by appearing more masculine, because they thought that by doing this men would take them more seriously on the job. They felt that this would provide a boost in their careers and receive a promotion or a raise in pay. These masculine tactics are still being used to this day.

This masculine change may explain why many women challenge men to competitions a lot more than they use to in the past. It may also explain why women don't want to be put in a feminine domestic role anymore, where they have to cook, clean the house and submit to a man because of the masculine culture that they have adopted. This adopted masculinity may also explain why women smoke and drink alcohol now more than ever in our history.

This also could explain why women are more aggressive and use bully tactics on men and fight more than they used to. A.K.A. "mean girls." This adopted masculinity may also explain why women have casual sex like a man and cheat more than men these days. There used to be a time when men cheated on their partners more than the women. Now, today's women have flipped this narrative around and now they cheat more than men these days.

This adopted masculinity may also explain why women will reject any or all things that put them in a feminine submissive role because they see or view femininity as weakness, because they are trying to equal men's masculinity in every way in order to compete with them. This may also explain why many women try to draw, bait or challenge men into a competition in order to prove a point that they are just as tough, strong and masculine as men.

Some of you may believe that this is a theory of "adopted masculinity" and not a reality and maybe debatable, but can you explain why women are more masculine now than ever? I'd love to hear an alternative answer to this question, but I don't think anyone can find a better, more logical answer than this one. Good luck finding it and if you do please enlighten me as I'm very interested in knowing about it.

Now, this adopted masculinity that women have taken on as part of their identity or who they are as a person, has gone unchecked and unchallenged and this explains why many men feel as if today's women treat them as if they should submit to them. Some women are okay with working outside the home, while the men stay at home and take care of the kids. A role reversal. Many women want to make men more feminine or at the very least they don't mind men becoming more feminine, that way they can take control in the relationship, just like a masculine man. Men—this would explain why your girlfriend, wife or someone you may be dating appears more masculine and unbalanced to you. Hmmm?

CHAPTER 9

ARE WOMEN SEXUALIZING THE WORKPLACE?

Dress for success

or

Dress to impress

The Magnet that attracts
SEXUAL ATTENTION

The forbidden fruit that creates a toxic work environment
that lures and entices the predators that—
SEXUALLY HARASS WOMEN

Why are some women targets for sexual harassment?
Some women are targeted for sexual harassment because they

are being viewed as sex objects and as easy to have sex with. A man picks and chooses a woman based upon how easy it is for him to have sex with her. No matter what you've been told from women or relationship therapists that a man wants a challenge in a woman; that's only if he wants to be in a relationship with her.

However, if a man wants to *only* have sex with a woman with no strings attached then he wants the easiest target that he can find. And according to men, it's a woman who is seeking sexual attention by the way she dresses. Remember that's all he has to go by at this point because he has no knowledge of who she is and nothing else to base it on when he first sees her.

A man figures the reason she is dressing so sexy is because she wants sexual attention. Therefore, he tests the waters and makes a sexual approach to see if that is the case. He then says something sexual to her in order to see if she takes the bait. If she takes the bait, meaning, she's open to sexual talk, and engages in a sexual conversation with him then he proceeds, but if she doesn't take the bait then he may be charged with sexual harassment. It's a high-risk game that he is playing, but it's also a 50/50 percent chance he could have sex with her. Yet his approach is all based on how she dresses.

Sexual clothes, used by women who dress sexy, triggers a "natural" sexual arousal in men. This behavior entices men to want to have sex with them, even if they don't want to have sex with them. If you don't believe that women who wear sexy clothes are a magnet to men's sexual arousal, then explain what makes a man attracted to a woman or how can a woman get a man to be attracted to her? The answer is makeup, hair and

SEXY CLOTHES!

She is trying to DRAW his interest and get him to like her without her having to say anything to him, because most women will not approach a man to express her interest, so she draws and attract his attention by the way she DRESSES, which makes her sexually attractive. When a woman wants to attract a man that she is interested in, she dresses as sexy as she can in order to entice him to her. Why? Because she knows that's the way to get his attention and to let him know that's she is interested in him.

For those women who say that clothes don't matter, would you go out on a date with a man that you really like and are interested in, looking like you just woke up out of bed? I'm sure the answer is *NO* for most of you. And why "no"? Because you know that he may lose interest in you. Right?

So, if the way one dresses can make a man lose interest in a woman, then can't it also make it a man gain interest in a woman? We all know the answer is yes! So, clothes do matter! And if those who still believe that sexy clothes don't matter, then explain why there are studies that show a billion-dollar industry based on selling sexual clothing that triggers men's natural arousal. Like Victoria's Secret.

You may say— but that's lingerie. My point is, that clothes are used as a sexual arousal tool. Otherwise, why don't women take off all of their clothes to arouse men in the private bedroom instead of using sex clothes to sexually arouse men? The answer is because women know that sexy clothing arouses men. So why are women and society saying that clothes have nothing to do with sexual harassment? I'm not say saying that sexy clothes make men sexually harass women.

However, I am saying that a woman's sexual dress draws the harasser's attention and entices him. Sexual clothing is the smoke that attracts the fire which is the harasser. There are different levels of harassers and harassment. There are the hardcore harassers which attack women physically. Then there are mid-level harassers which use verbal vulgarity when talking to women. And then there are the lower-level harassers who badger women for dates even though the women keep turning them down.

However, the one thing that all three harassers have in common is that they all are attracted to the woman whose dress is sexually appealing. And for those women who say that how a woman dresses has nothing to do with harassment is turning a blind eye to the obvious. Human nature cannot be denied. Sexual nature and sexual attraction which is brought upon by attention-seeking through dressing sexually appealing is a reality too.

And to say that the way someone dresses has nothing to do with sexual harassment is simply ludicrous. It may not be the main reason why men harass women, but it is one of the reasons why men harass women. Therefore, we have to take that into account when evaluating sexual harassment on the job so that we can stop sexual harassment on the job or in the workplace.

If we continue to dismiss this aspect of sexual harassment and sexually dressed women on the job, then we will never solve the issues and problem of sexual harassment. I know some of you are saying, "but you are blaming women for sexual harassment."

I'm not blaming women for the creep who actually sexually harassed them, but I am making women realize they are sexualizing the workplace by the way they dress. Women who dress sexy on the job are making a conscious decision and choice to draw sexual attention to themselves, which creates a sexually toxic workplace environment, because it draws the attention of the creepy harassers.

There are men who can look at a sexually dressed women and it wouldn't bother them at all. Still, these women have to take into account the creepy guy who's looking for an opportunity to harass women. Women can't control the creepy harassers. However, they can control the way they dress and in turn, take away any reasons for sexual harassers to harass them based upon how they dress.

Like I said, men harass women for different reasons and one of the reasons is that some men believe that a woman who dresses sexy on the job or at the workplace is looking for sexual attention like the female waitress or bartender who expose their cleavages in order to draw sexual attention to themselves for a bigger tip.

Men don't know the difference between two women who dress for different reasons because they both look identical. Especially when many of today's women wear night club clothes to the office. For example, they'll wear extra short and tight fitted dresses with cleavage showing in order to draw attention to themselves, in order to get a self-esteem boost.

That's an example of sexualizing the workplace. And some of you still don't believe that sexy clothes have an impact or that it matters? Then explain why after a date or night on the town, why a woman puts on sexy lingerie? Because she knows that this would trigger a man's natural sexual arousal.

Explain why a wife who wants to get sexual attention from her husband, puts on sexy clothes or lingerie in order to put him in the mood to have sex with her. Explain why some women dress sexy to go out to a night club in order to engage or attract men to them and in some cases have a one-night stand.

These examples are proven facts that sexy clothes attract and arouse men sexually. So, when a woman wears sexy clothes at the workplace or on the job, she is indirectly triggering sexual arousal and putting men in the mood to want to have sex with her. Explain why a waitress or female bartender wears sexy tops exposing their cleavage or part of their breasts? It's in order to draw a man's sexual attention and to trigger his sexual arousal so that he would be nice to her and give her a bigger tip (money).

We all know that sex sells. Why? Because it triggers the sexual arouses in men. When men get sexually aroused then they are more friendly and generous towards women, because they want to have sex with them. It's a natural instinct that can't be defied by artificial professionalism. Professionalism is manmade. It's pretended, not real and virtual reality. It's not natural, therefore it will never trump or replace natural sexual instincts.

Women wear sexy clothes on the job in order to get attention and validation (which makes them feel good about themselves), from both men and women. Validating women gives them a self-esteem boost, which they need because many women have low self-esteem and wearing sexy clothing is their way of getting that self-esteem boost. However, at the same time wearing sexy clothes triggers a man's natural sexual arousal, which would cause men to view women in a sexual way, which makes men want to have sex with these sexually dressed and enticing women.

Therefore, it makes many men want to approach these sexually dressed and enticing women in order to see if they would date them and eventually have sex with them. I know there are some women saying that clothes don't cause sexual harassment, it is the men who committed the act that actually cause sexual harassment. You are correct except the fact that women are wearing sexually enticing clothes, like tight fitting body dresses fit for a night club but not the workplace.

Women wearing low cut tops showing their cleavage. Women wearing short skirts or dresses that are mid-thigh and two inches from showing their vagina. These are all sexually enticing clothing designed and calculated to draw attention and sexually arouse men. The only problem is that it is worn in the wrong places and those are the places where many women don't want men's sexual attention because it may bring on sexual harassment or assault, which we all hear about.

If you don't believe this, then explain why waitresses and female bar tenders wear sexy clothing on the job showing their cleavage? We all know it's to draw sexual attention to the men patronage or customers so that these men will view these women in a sexual way or sexual object (which is conflicting because women say they shouldn't be viewed as sexual objects) so that they would manipulate the men to falsely believe that they have a chance to have sex with them.

If that's the case, then why do many people think wearing sexy clothes would have a different effect in the office or other workplace environment? It doesn't, and that's one of the main reasons why there is sexual harassment in the workplace. It's not the only reason, but it's a major reason. I'm not saying that women should get harassed because they wear sexy clothing, but I am saying that women who wear sexy clothes on the job do so in order to draw or get attention for their own self esteem boost, and this is sexually enticing to men, which is human nature and just because they are in a professional setting does not and will not eliminate a man's natural instincts to be attracted to a sexy women.

The best he can do is try to suppress his own feelings about it, but it won't stop it in general. Therefore, women who don't want to be sexually harassed have to be conscious and cautious of how they dress at work if they don't want to draw sexual attention or be sexually harassed. Remember, not every man is moral and upstanding. There are some mental cases and creeps out there that are waiting on an opportunity to harass or assault women.

So, it's up to the women to protect themselves. And one way is to not draw toxic sexual attention to themselves by wearing sexy night club clothes to a daytime workplace. All types of dress have their own separate place. It's similar to a woman who walks down a dark alley by herself. I know that women should be free to do what they want to do in today's society. However, some things are just not smart for a woman to do even though she is free to do it.

A woman who walks down a dark alley alone at night is putting herself at risks for being attacked or sexually assaulted. Just like a woman who wear night club clothes at the office is putting herself in jeopardy to be sexually harassed, not by sane men but the creepy nutcases that she can't control or hadn't accounted for. This is why women shouldn't wear a bikini to an office job. Why not? Because it's inappropriate.

Why is it inappropriate? Because a woman would draw unwanted sexual attention to herself, which is toxic to her and the workplace. So why are some wearing sexy night club clothes to their daytime job? Wouldn't it still be inappropriate and drawing unwanted sexual attention to yourself? If so, then what makes you think that a man wouldn't view a woman as a sexual object and approach her sexually in that case? Just because she is at work? Makes no sense.

If you have on sexy night club clothes on the daytime job or at nighttime and off work, remember you are still the same person and you still look sexy to a man. Just because a woman's physical location has changed doesn't mean that a man's sexual instincts and arousal have changed. He is still a man and you are still a woman, and a man is going to always be attracted to a sexy woman no matter what location she is in.

I know that this is no excuse for him to say anything inappropriate to a woman, but my having to say this alone says that there is something about the woman that's causing him say something inappropriate. Meaning, the way she dresses. Now most women still believe that a man should be professional on the job no matter if this woman is dressing sexy or not. I get that point.

However just because women want men to suppress their emotions and feelings about a sexually dressed woman, doesn't mean that men would do it. Trying to make men suppress their natural instincts, which includes their attraction to a scantily dressed woman, is not feasible. Because the only way for a man to get to know a woman or be in a relationship with her is for him to be sexually attracted to her and to approach her. How will that happen if a man's feelings are suppressed? Most dating relationship starts at work, A.K.A. an office romance.

Some people have even married their workplace partners. Tying to defy human nature by being too "professional" will not work now or never. Therefore, if women don't want that sexual attention then they have to tone down on some of the over-the-top scantily clad styles at the workplace. You are never going to stop a man from desiring scantily clad women. Men are visually stimulated.

If the women who dress this way don't want that sexual attention, why are they dressing sexy on the job when they know a man may view or approach them in a sexual way? Women need to take some of the accountability for creating a sexualized workplace environment. Dressing sexy on the job sexualizes the job. And sexualizing the workplace by their dressing to attract sexual attention is 100% the women's fault.

But the sexual harassment itself is 100% the men's fault because they took the bait. The bait in this instance means the women wanting sexual attention but without men approaching them sexually. Many women want it both ways. They want men's attention by the way they dress but they don't want men to say anything to them sexually on the job. This results in a conflict that sends mixed messages.

Women want the attention for their own self esteem boost, but they don't want the men's attention for the men's own sexual boost. So how will a man know if a woman wants him to approach her or not? He doesn't and that's where the conflict and the sexual harassment comes in. Therefore, women need to stop sending mixed signals and stop sexualizing the workplace if they see sex harassment as a major problem.

There is a saying, "be careful what you ask for because you just might get it." Women seek sexual attention by the way they dress on the job, then once they get it, they complain about it. It's like when a woman comes home from work and starts to complain to her husband or boyfriend about all of the problems that she is having at work and then gets upset with him because he is trying to come up with solutions and answers for her. She then tells him that she didn't ask him for his advice or solutions, she just wanted him to listen to her.

Men don't understand that logic from women. Men think that she is telling him about her problems because she wants him to help solve her problems, otherwise why bother him with her stress. I believe that this is the same mentality when women dress sexy on the job.

Women want the men's sexual attention but don't want them to comment or tell her what he thinks or how he really feels about it. This is strange behavior to men. Women should be clearer and stop complaining because men can't read their minds. Men are not mind readers or interpreters. Women can't have it both ways. I believe that women should stop sexualizing the workplace by not dressing sexy and to start dressing appropriately and professional.

I have a question for those who believe that women should wear whatever they want, and nobody should tell them how to dress. What's appropriate clothing on the job? Is it okay for a woman to wear a G-string and high heels to the office? I'm sure the answer is no. But why not? It's still clothes. Her private parts are covered. But some of you say that a woman can wear whatever she wants to at work. But it doesn't seem so appropriate now. Why not? Because she may get sexually harassed or assaulted?

But why would that happen? I thought some of you said that clothes don't make men harass women. We all know that it is because she is going too far for you. What's too far and who gets to decide? This is why there needs to be some kind of standard on the job (set by the business owner or management) because many women have pushed the envelope to the edge of inappropriateness and it has cause a spike in sexual attention, which has crosses the line to sexually harassment.

Therefore, the way one dresses *does* matter, and has an indirect effect upon sexual harassment. If you still don't believe that the way a woman dresses has an indirect effect on sexual harassment, then I'm sure it's okay to you for women to wear whatever they want to work and that includes just wearing a thong and bra? Yeah right!

This attitude is just a way for some of you women to take any scrutiny or blame off of yourselves for sexualizing the workplace, which in some cases (but not all) leads to sexual harassment on the job. Some of you may not like that I said that, or accept that fact but it's true, because you still can't justify it is appropriate for a woman to wear just a G-string and heels to the office.

Remember it's still clothing, and her private parts are covered. Therefore sexualizing the workplace, by wearing sexy night club clothes on the job is inappropriate because it indirectly leads to sexual attention, which leads to sexual approaches, which leads to sexual harassment if the woman doesn't want the man to comment on only her sexy clothes. So, let's keep it real!

CHAPTER 10

#WeToo Movement

What is the #WeToo Movement?

The #WeToo Movement is a movement of men who were falsely accused of sexual assault or harassment by women.

"We too have been falsely accused."

Men are joining together to stop, shame and punish women for falsely accusing men of sexual assault or harassment. Men are saying that they are not going to take it anymore. They will not be shamed, intimidated, bully or railroaded by women who falsely accused them. That is the gist of this movement.

If women are going to be allowed to accuse men of the crime of sexual assault or harassment (without proof or evidence) then men have no choice but to advocate having women locked up and put in jail for falsely accusing them of a sexual assault or harassment claim.

Women would have to prove their case of sexual assault or harassment with physical evidence or some kind of other proof and if they don't have the proof or evidence, then don't bring the case to the justice system, otherwise men should be allowed to have the women brought up on charges for filing a false police report or charge of criminal wrongdoing.

This is the countermovement to balance the #MeToo Movement. A woman shouldn't just be allowed to totally destroy a man's life, make him lose his job and his family without any proof or evidence to back up her claim. It should not be based on her word "alone". Everything in our court and justice system requires the burden of "proof", and women and the #MeToo Movement are NO exception.

Why are we giving women a free pass to destroy a man's life with no facts, no proof or anything to back it up but her "word"? As if women don't lie, and only men lie. Women have faults and flaws just like men. This is the reason that we have to have proof or evidence to back up any claims. Something that serious has to be taken very seriously. I know that some of you are saying, "women should just be believed."

Okay, if you feel that way then let me ask you a question: Do women lie? Or are they holier than thou and pure as the driven snow with no faults and flaws? Perfect?

We all know the answer to the first question is YES! Women lie too. As long as women lie and are capable of falsely accusing a man of sexual assault or harassment then we as a society MUST require proof of very serious accusations or otherwise don't bring the claim or charges to a legal setting, or these women will be challenged and charged in court with falsely accusing a man.

Some of you might be saying that this will discourage women from coming forward. If a woman has proof or some kind of evidence, she shouldn't have a problem and she won't get charged because she has that evidence. It doesn't have to be a smoking gun proof, but it at least has to be circumstantial evidence, something where we can weigh the pros and cons in order to make a reasonable assessment of the situation.

Otherwise don't bring a claim from years or decades ago with a woman's word only. Otherwise men have every right to bring a false accusation charge against her. This is the balance that is needed for accusing a man with no evidence or proof to back it up. Now if the woman has proof, even circumstantial proof is good enough, as long as there is something to back up their claim, and not just their word alone, this should be enough to go by.

Women ask for equality and now they are going to get it. For those who still want to see men punished for a very serious accusation and crime, without proof or evidence, and destroy a man's life, even though this woman could be lying, you are a setting a very dangerous precedent. There is a saying, be careful what you ask for because you just might get it.

Women have been asking for equality for a while and now they have it. The accusations and criminal charges go both ways. If a woman falsely accuses a man of sexual assault or harassment, then she should expect to be criminally charged. Men will no longer be a punching bag for women just like women will not tolerate being a punching bag for men. That's equality and what the #We Too Movement is all about.

CHAPTER 11

MEN FALSELY ACCUSED

Men are Collateral Damage!
So What!?—Who Cares about you and your Rights!

Men Falsely Accused of Sexual Assault

A few years back some of the Duke Lacrosse team players were at a party with some strippers having fun like college kids sometimes do. They were drinking and watching the strippers do their thing, which is to strip. Well, I guess one of the strippers got upset for whatever reason and called the police and reported a rape. She said that the guys had sexual assaulted her and raped her. The guys were immediately stopped from participating in sporting events and thrown off of the team. All without any evidence except for the woman's word that they commit his crime.

The media instantly vilified them. The school had shut

down their fraternity house. They had to pay for and get lawyers because they were facing some serious jail time. It took years of their lives walking around with everyone thinking they were rapists. After the smoke had cleared, the charges were dropped, because it turn out that they were telling the truth and that the woman had lied. They were completed exonerated by the court.

Now after all of that stress the men went through and the anxiety of potentially going to jail and ruining their lives over a lie, what do you think happened to the woman who made the false accusation? You guessed it, absolutely nothing! That's right, she got off scot-free after ruining these guys reputation and destroying their lives which will never be the same again. She got no punishment for her actions. That's disgraceful. In other words, she weaponized sex through a false sexual assault claim, and got no punishment for her crime. There was no fairness or equality and justice for the guys whom she put through hell. So, men wake up, because—there's a price to pay!

CHAPTER 12

MY PERSONAL STORY

Being falsely accused is very personal to me because I have my own personal experience at being falsely accused. Yes, I too, was falsely accused of rape. It was in the mid-nineties and I was in a relationship with a woman who was almost ten years older than me at the time. I was in my late twenties and I was going through a divorce. I was young and I was dating because I didn't know what I wanted at the time. So I kept my options open.

She was Filipina and very, very needy and clingy. She wanted to be with me every day, all day. I thought she was too smothering. I also thought some of her behavior was very strange. I would get up in the morning to use the bathroom and she would be waiting outside the door on me to come out. She didn't have to use the bathroom, she just wanted to be near me in the house. Strange, huh? I thought so too.

One day we had went to Home Depot and I had forgotten something in the car, and I asked her to go get it for me. I think it was my wallet. Well, she took a long time and it stuck in my mind wondering as to why it took so long. This part is very important for later. Okay, then months had gone by and we were dating with nothing major going on. But before that, I used to come home from work, and she would be on my porch waiting for me to come home.

Now understand that I didn't invite her over and I didn't know that she was coming over either. She would do this two to three times a week. Yeah, I thought that was a little strange, too. She'd be waiting outside until I got home, not knowing what time I was going to come home or even if I would come home. Then after some time went by, I started noticing that things in my house would be missing or moved around. Sometimes I would come home and if I put the phone on the charger before I left and went to work then it would be off the chart when I got back home.

Then I would come home, and I would smell food as if some had been cooking in my house. On other occasions I would come home from work again, I would see small things out of place, and I know I didn't move them. Now granted, I was dating her, but I was also dating another girl too, because we weren't exclusive, so I felt that I had every right to do so. Did I tell her? No. Hey I was young and was keeping my options open. We all make mistakes; I may have been wrong. I'm quite sure you have made some mistakes too.

So, don't judge me. He who is without sin cast the first stone! Anyway. One day I was at the other girl's house around seven or eight o'clock. Then as we both were sitting there talking and watching television, her phone rang. So, she looked at the caller ID and turned to look at me and asked, "why is somebody calling me from your house?" I said, "what do you mean, my house." She said isn't this your phone number, and showed me the number on the caller ID. I said, "damn, you're right." I called my own number back and a person answered the phone but quickly hung up. Okay, this scared the *shit* out of me.

So, I immediately call the police and reported a burglary. Then I got up and drove to my house and when I got there the girl that I had mentioned first that I was dating was in my house. I asked her what was she doing there and how in the hell she got into my house? She didn't answer me at that time. She was just very upset and started yelling and cursing at me. Remember, I had called the police, and they were on their way. I had beat them to my house.

So, her and I were arguing back and forth, and then she said that she was going to call the police on me. I said, "for what!?" She called anyway and just said that she wanted them to come. At the same time the police I had called were coming up the stairs to address the burglary that I had reported before. She didn't know that I had called the police already. So, she heard the police coming up the stairs to enter the house, she tried to tear her night gown that she had on (remember I didn't know that she was in my house). I guess she was planning to surprise me.

However, she couldn't tear the night gown with her own hands, so she ran into the kitchen and got a knife and cut it. She

124

made a slit right down the middle of the night gown. When the cops entered the house, she ran up to them and said, "he raped me!" I was stunned at the accusation because I know I didn't rape her because I wasn't even there, and I was with another woman at that time. "What the hell are you talking about!?" I demanded to know. I hadn't had sex with her for at least a month, because we were going through bad times and we were about to break up anyway.

The officers approached her and said, "I thought we were here to investigate a burglary?" She said, "no, I called you." I said "no, I called them before I got here because I didn't know who was in my house." So now we had a standoff with two different sets of police because now the other set of police officers had arrived. So, then I ask for the sergeant to come and settle this matter. We are all waiting on the sergeant and he finally gets there. Then we are talking, and he asks whose phone call came in first. They checked it and mine had come in first.

Then they ask me what happen to her night gown, because it was torn. I said "that's not torn, that's cut." I said that she tried to tear it, but she couldn't, so she went and got a knife a cut it. I said, "look at it that's a cut." They said, "it sure is." So I got on the phone and called my ex-wife, the mother of my kids, and told her what was happening and if could she come over there, because she knew about the girl. They once had an argument.

While I was waiting on my ex, the female police officer had said to me that they believe that she is lying. She said, "I have a son your age so I'm going to stick with you because they will try to lock you up." In the meantime, I was walking around my house waiting on my ex to come, and she finally got there. While I was sitting down, I said to the sergeant, "look at me, do I look like I just raped someone?" I said, "do I look scared or nervous to you." I said to him, "sergeant, you are not a stupid person, you didn't get that white shirt for nothing," because sergeants wear white shirts to help others differentiate them from other police officers. That's how you know who's in charge.

While everyone was trying to figure out what to do, I had to use the bathroom. As I was about enter the bathroom, I saw her clothes had been folded up and was on my hamper that was in the bathroom. So, I went and got the sergeant and asked to him to look at her clothes. He asked, "what about them?" I said, "look at them, they are folded up" I said, "are you telling me that I rape someone and then folded up their clothes." Then the sergeant asked her how her clothes got folded up.

She responded, "huh?" as if she didn't understand him. So, I asked the sergeant to ask her where the rape took place. She said, "in the bedroom." What I was doing was setting her up by locking in her statement so that she can't change it. Because I knew I didn't rape her. So again, I asked the sergeant to ask her how we have sex? Did use a condom or unprotected? He asked and she said "unprotected."

Well, while I was talking to the sergeant, my ex had gone into the kitchen and she found the knife that my accuser had cut her night gown with. So, she goes to tell the police to come look at it. It still had the fibers in it from her night gown. When my accuser told the sergeant that I was unprotected, and didn't use a condom, I said to myself, "got her." Then I said to the officers, "you can take me down to the police station." They then took me out in handcuffs, and they had the woman come to file the complaint.

After that they asked me to have the other girl that I was with that night to bring her caller ID so that they can view to see when did the calls came in. Now, we are all at the police station and I was there a total ten minutes and I heard this loud screaming. They had me in a holding room. Within ten seconds of me hearing the screaming the officers let me out and told me that I can go home. I asked them what happened. They said that they believed that she was lying and if she didn't admit it and tell the truth that they would lock her up for making a false police report.

So, she confessed to everything. She told them that she made up the story because she was angry that I was with the other girl. Also, she told them how she got into my house, and how she got the girl's phone number to call that night. Now remember, I didn't know how she got into my house. Well, she told the police how she got into my house and this is how she did it.

Remember I told you about that incident at Home Depot which had stuck in my mind? Well, the reason why she took so long getting back to the car when I asked her to go get something for me, was because she had taken my keys and went and had a duplicate copy made. She said told the police that she was tired of waiting outside of my house, when I was at work. So, she had a key made so that she could get in and didn't have to wait outside in the cold.

Now everything made sense to me. She was coming in and out of my house while I was at work. That explained all of the items that went missing and things that were moved around in my house, which made me think that I was crazy or had ghosts or something. Now that you have heard my personal story where I was falsely accused of rape, what should her punishment or consequence need to have been for her actions?

She got a free pass from trying to have me locked up just because she was angry that I was with another girl. That's a terrible way to use to police and the justice system against a man. She did because, she knew will go, unchecked, and unchallenged. Also, she knew that there would be no consequences for her actions, which is her taking advantage of being a woman! So again, I ask of you, what should a woman's punishment or consequence be for falsely accusing a man of sexual assault or rape?

CHAPTER 13

THE SEXUAL GATEKEEPERS: WHO'S THE BOSS?

Women Dictate—Determine & Control All Consenting
Sexual Activities

When-Where-With-Whom, And Why—Until she Says YES,
the Answer is NO!

What is a sexual gatekeeper? A sexual gatekeeper is a woman who is in charge of her body. She is responsible for what happens to it because she is in control. Women are in control, in charge and responsible for all sexual activity between a man and a woman, with the exception of forced assault.

Without a woman's consent, sex does not take place. A woman has to agree and give a man permission in order to touch her body in a sexual way. A man could want to have sex with her all he wants to, but until she consents and agrees, a man has no right to touch her in anyway sexually. Therefore, all responsibility lies at the woman's feet, but (many women try to shift that responsibility or accountability to men or blame others when things go wrong or when it doesn't favor them).

Sometimes this great sexual power is abused and used against men. Some women hold men hostage to its power. What do I mean by that? Seventy percent of women initiate the breakups between men and women. The reasons for these breakups are all based on anything that the women feel that don't suit them or favors their positions. It can go from something major or something petty, like money to sex, or some as simple as the woman was just "bored".

Why would a woman break up a good relationship because she is "bored"? It's because she has the sexual power to easily get another man to replace the old one. This power over sex has spoiled and given women a sense of entitlement over relationships, to the point where anything they do has to favor them or it's no longer desirable.

Women know and understand the power over sex that they have and will use it to their advantage whenever and however they can. Many women will abuse their power as the sexual gatekeeper to manipulate and deceive men into giving them whatever they want like money, gifts, or a luxury lifestyle.

However, this is a double-edged sword for women because they have to take the good with the bad and the positive with the negative. What do I mean by that? Women give themselves and men the pleasures of enjoying sex. However, she is the one who gets to decide which particular man gets to enjoy her body. So, she must be very careful with the choices she makes. If she has bad judgment and chooses the wrong partner, then she will get hurt and suffer the consequences because of that choice.

He could just want to have sex with her and leave her with no comment to be in a relationship with her. In other words, he would just use her for his own selfish pleasures. Also, with a bad decision she could get a sexually transmitted disease (STD), like HIV and she could be putting her life in danger if she exercises bad judgment and doesn't use protection like condoms. In addition, she could have an unplanned pregnancy and be left with another tough decision of whether or not to have an abortion and end the pregnancy.

In all these cases the choices are hers to make, and hers alone because she is the sexual gatekeeper and is 100% in control of her body and what happens to it, and the decisions with whom to have sexual contact. The man has no part in her decision-making process. It is hers and hers alone. I know you are probably thinking, well, why doesn't the man have a role in this situation because it takes two to make a baby or he could give her a STD.

That's true, he could get her pregnant or give her a STD but it's still her choice and her decision to have sex with him, and if she hadn't done her homework properly and checked him out to see if he is the right guy for her, before she has sex with him or, if she rushed into having sex with him then it's still her fault because it was her choice to give in to his advances and give him permission to have sex with her.

You may say, well what if she is young and immature. It's still her body and she is still responsible for what happens to her body. And if she is immature, then she shouldn't be having sex if she doesn't understand the consequences and repercussions of her actions. It is still 100% her fault. Why? Because she could have easily said no just like she said yes!

But she didn't, so she has to suffer the consequences of her bad judgment because, if she doesn't agree to have sex with him then sex doesn't happen, and if sex doesn't happen then she doesn't get pregnant or get an STD regardless of what he thinks about it because it's her body and she gets to decide what to do with it.

Therefore, she has to be wiser with her choice of men. If you still think that a man is part responsible for giving her a STD or an unplanned pregnancy, then let me ask you this question. Who's responsible for abortions the man or the woman? I'm sure you just said the woman. Why can't a man make the decision of abortion for a woman? I'm quite sure you will say because it's her choice and her choice alone because it's her body and she gets to decide what happens to her body and not a man. Right? Are we on the same page at this point? Good.

Okay, if that the case then—wasn't it her body in the beginning before she made the decision to have sex with a man and also, before the decision that led to the STD and the unplanned pregnancy? Of course, it was. So why do you think it is 100% her right in the end when it comes to abortion, because it's her body, but you don't think it's 100% her decision in the beginning when she made the decision to have unprotected sex?

It's interesting that some of you feel that way. That she somehow gave up 50% of her choices to the man when it came to pregnancy, but she gets the have 100% of the choice when it comes to abortion. You can't have it both ways. You must choose. Is it her body or not? If the answer is yes, then she is 100% responsible for the sex that occurs, and she has to take 100% of the blame because it's her body and her choice before and after pregnancy.

Or do you think that men should share the decision with her and responsibility of sex and then they both get to make the decision for her to let him have sex with her anytime he wants to? I'm sure you are probably saying no to that too. Why? Because men don't get to make a decision to have sex with a woman unless she consents to it right? So, if that's the case, then and he has no say or choice in the matter or situation at all—It's all her decision, right?

If so, then why isn't it all her fault? It is all her responsibility because it's all choices and decisions that *she* made, and she made them *alone*. I know that a lot of women don't like to hear this but it's true. The reason women don't want to hear this is because they don't want to take accountability for their actions or for things that went wrong from the bad choices and decisions that they made.

They want the men to share or take all of the blame, which gives women a free pass. They want the men to take the burden of things gone wrong off of them. However, at the same time they want to take credit for the positive choices and decisions they make. In other words, they want it both ways. When it favors them it's their choice but when it doesn't favor them then it's a shared responsibility or entirely the man's fault and makes him take the blame for any negative outcomes.

Women in this day and age can no longer blame men for their bad judgment, however, because they are strong, independent women who are equal to men in every way and also, they are the sexual gatekeepers and all sexual decisions and choices go through them.

I'm old enough to remember when there use to be a time when a woman could blame a man for getting her drunk and taking advantage of her. When things went wrong she would say things like, "he got me drunk" as if she had no part in her getting herself drunk and that somehow the man must have poured or forced the alcohol down her throat. She would say that because she didn't want to take responsibility for her bad behavior or negative actions.

So, she would play little Miss Innocent in order to get herself out of trouble but at the same time, would blame the man and make him take the fall for her bad judgment. Since women enjoy being the sexual gatekeepers, they would treat similar behavior as with the alcohol excuse. In other words, blame men and let them take the fall for the negative outcomes and actions of the woman.

What do I mean by this? If a woman gets pregnant, then she would say that, "he got me pregnant" as if she had no part or say so in her getting herself pregnant and somehow he forced her to get pregnant against her will. When in fact the entire decision to have unprotected sex was all hers. How?

Because she could have easily declined him because he didn't have protection.

However, in our example, she didn't say "no"—and therefore she allowed him, gave consent and permission to him to have unprotected sex with her. But if she didn't agree to have sex unprotected—then sex wouldn't have happened, because he wasn't going to force himself onto her. He would have to wait for her permission, which means it all comes down to her choice and her decision, otherwise sex wouldn't have happened.

I know you're probably thinking or saying to yourself that I'm putting all the blame on the woman and giving the man a free pass and letting him off the hook scot-free. He's at least partly responsible because it takes two to make a baby. Right? Don't worry he's not getting a free pass trust me. He will be held accountable like all men are! Men don't get free passes when it comes to their negative behavior. Men will have to pay child support or go to jail for not paying. Therefore, he will be held accountable for his part in this situation. Unlike the women.

Women's sexual irresponsibility can no longer be ignored or tolerated by men or women anymore because women are the sexual gatekeepers, and all choices and decision about having sex is 100% (with the exception of forced assaults) their responsibility or fault.

I know being the sexual gatekeeper carries with it a heavy burden and responsibility, however this is the hand that women have been dealt with and given, just like child birth, it's the hand that women were given (to bare children) that men can't have, so women have to deal with it in a moral and responsible way and if it's not handled properly then women and women alone have to deal with the consequences of their actions as the sexual gatekeeper.

CHAPTER 14

USING SEX TO GET WHAT SHE WANTS: THE CONTROL WEAPON THAT'S USED AGAINST MEN

Being the sexual gatekeeper in a relationship is used as a control weapon where women can use sex against men, to demand, and take advantage of, or use it in a manipulative way. What do I mean by that? I mean that many women use sex to manipulate men into getting their way or to get things that they want. Some women will withhold sex from men until they give in to their demands. Why? Because most women know that a man's need for sex is one of his top priorities besides money.

Therefore, many women will use this need against a man in order to get financial gain or some other thing that's important to the woman, out of the situation. Money is a motivating factor for many women when it comes to a man or relationship. Most women will not get into a relationship if a man cannot provide for them financially, even if they can provide for themselves. They know that men will give them things in exchange for sex.

This does not mean it's a direct transaction as in prostitution, but it'll be more like some kind of favor. Women, being the sexual gatekeepers will use their sexual power in order to demand that a man do or give something in exchange for their bodies, that is, if the man wants something sexual from them. They will make a man take them out to dinners, movies some or form of entertainment, give them gifts or cash money in exchange for sex. Otherwise he will not get sex from them based only on his words.

This is how women have transformed sex into a weapon against men. For many women sex is used as a bargaining chip rather than for pleasure. If you don't believe it, then ask any women if they will have sex with or enter a relationship with a man if he is broke and down on his luck or won't provide for them monetarily or material-wise. I guarantee you that ninety 90% of the women will say "no", and they will not be willing to enter into a sexual relationship with such a man.

This reminds me of a famous song by TLC, the girl hip-hop group. The song was called *No Scrubs.* The gist of the song was about a broke guy who has no money, and why they wouldn't get with him, explaining that they wouldn't have sex with him because he has no money. Also, they won't want to get into a relationship with him because he is broke and has no money to take care of them.

That's how the majority of women feel about a man, even

though they are independent and can provide for themselves. They believe that because they are the sexual gatekeepers, that they are doing men a favor by providing sex for them, therefore they want something in return for that sexual favor. Something other than just a sex for sex exchange. Meaning a penis for a vagina.

When a man is first introduced to a woman, one of the first things she will ask of him is "what kind of work do you do" or "what do you do for a living". Why do women ask these kinds of question to men? They ask these questions because they are sizing him up to see if he would be a good provider for them or their children. It's their way of eliminating or excluding the unqualified candidates without their knowledge or tipping their hand as to what they truly want him for (which is money).

The sexual gatekeeper knows the value of her body and she will use it to get what's most important or desirable to her, even though she has her own money, car, house, etc. Don't believe it? Then why do women ask about a man's job or work when they first meet. Is it just because they are interested? I don't think so and neither do you.

We all know what that is about: potential money for her. Why do women say that they had a bad date if they guy took them to McDonald's? They complain that he was very cheap because they want him to spend more money on them because they don't want to give up sex for such a small price because it makes them look as if they have no worthy or value. They want to feel like they are worth something more to a man. They want to feel like their sexual favor is worth more than just a burger and some fries from McDonald's. They don't want to feel cheap like a whore.

They intend to get something worthwhile for their sexual favor if they decide to give it to him. The sexual gatekeepers know their value and they are looking for a certain type of lifestyle in exchange for that sexual value. The sexual gatekeepers have the power to create and the power to destroy.

She had the power to create a relationship and life (by conceiving a baby) or the power to destroy them (such as through abortion). That's why they are always seeking the highest value male that they can find. Because they know that all relationships for women and the core of their lives goes through them as the sexual gatekeepers. Most women are opportunists and they seek a certain lifestyle, which is what a man can do for them, and not a relationship.

Why? Because as the sexual gatekeepers they can have sex anytime they want to because they have the power over sex and men do not. Therefore, they use it to their advantage. In other words, they weaponize sex, by getting as much value as they can from a man in exchange for the sexual favor that they can provide.

So, for men there will always be a price they have to pay for the sexual favors from the sexual gatekeepers. However, it's a double-edged sword for women. Women—A word of advice, if you misuse this great power over sex that you have been given by the Creator, just remember, that you are not the only sexual gatekeeper on the planet, there's plenty of competition and there is always another sexual gatekeeper looking to replace you! Hmmm? Therefore, use it wisely or men will just move on to the next one. Men have an abundance of choices too, even more because there are more women than men in the world. Life have a way of keeping all things fair, equal and balanced.

Chapter 15

Weaponizing Sex/Sexual Assault and Harassment:

NEGATIVE EMPOWERMENT

Intimidation and Bullying Tactics used in Order Control
and Gain an Advantage over Men!

What is weaponizing sex?

Weaponizing sex is when a woman uses sex to hurt, dominate, tear down, destroy, take away, manipulate, shame, intimidate, bully, and so on in order to gain an advantage over the men in their lives.

Men—have you ever had a woman use her sex appeal and flirt with or tease you in order to get money or a gift from you or to gain some kind of advantage over you but never really had any intentions of ever having sex with you?

For example: I've been to numerous restaurants in my life where I see female waitresses flirt with male customers. They pretend as if they are interested in the men as some (not all) dress provocatively, teases them, smile and wink at them with the intent of leading them on sexually. They do this sexual manipulation in order to get a higher tip from the man. However, the women know that he has a zero chance to get with them sexually.

The female waitresses who flirt with their male customers have NO intent on having sex with them, and they are just trying to use their sex appeal to get a bigger tip from them. However in this day and age with the "#MeToo" movement, it's a very dangerous game for men that these women are playing with them, because if he takes her seriously then he could end up in a lot of legal trouble both criminally and financially, if he flirts back or crosses the line in her eyes.

The potential sexual assault would then be viewed and based only on how the woman feels about the situation and not the men's intent even though it is the woman who is the person who is injecting the sexual aspect into the conversation or situation. That's weaponizing sex.

Here's what I mean. The woman starts the flirting and sexual innuendos. She gets to determine where the line gets drawn even for him. Therefore, she can flirt with him, but he can't flirt back unless she gives him permission to do so. She gets to make the rules for the sexually charged game that she is playing. If she touched him in a sexual way and he touched her back in a sexual way, then who is the sexual assault victim?

Him or her? I'm quite sure the majority of people would say *her*.

She is the victim. But why is she the victim and not him? They both touch each other in an inappropriate way. So why does she get a free pass and he gets a potentially jail sentence if she complains to the police. There is only one answer available, and that because she is a woman and he is a man. I know there are some of you saying that he should have kept his hand to himself then he wouldn't have had a problem.

However, it's interesting that no one said that she should've kept her hands to herself. Why not? Because women have been given a pass when it comes to them sexually harassing men. That's weaponizing sex, right there.

I remember a famous case where a female schoolteacher and a teenager male student in her class, had a sexual affair. He was underage and the older female teacher had gotten pregnant by the underaged student. They sent her to jail for statutory rape because he was a minor. However, the news coverage of the ordeal consisted of people trying to get her off the hook and blaming the young boy.

They were saying things like "he must have liked it." Meaning, he must have liked having sex with an older woman. And they tried to make her out to be the victim in this case because she was a woman. Now, if the places were reversed and this had been an older man with a teenage underaged girl, then everyone would've been saying, lock him up and throw away the key. However, because she was female, they wanted the justice system to go easy on her and give her a get out of jail free pass.

Why the double standard with sex, when it comes to men and women? If women believe that we live in an equal society, why are they okay being treated as victims and men treated as villains? This is the kind of double standard has made it easy for some women to weaponize sex against men. As long as a woman believes that she will get a free pass because of her gender then this will inspire many of them to do something malicious. This is what happens when women are unchecked, and unchallenged. It causes a shift in the balance between men and women, and also cause many women to believe that they are entitled to get a free pass and take advantage of being a woman.

For example: Women—have you ever dressed sexy in the workplace? If so, why? Who are you trying to impress on the job? A male coworker? If so why? Are you flirting on the job? If so, why? Are you dating someone on the job? If so, why? Some of you are probably thinking, "what's wrong with women dressing up for themselves in order to feel good about themselves?"

I ask these questions of women because the workplace is the most dangerous place for women to inject sexuality. Simply because of all of the sexual harassment claims and lawsuits. If a woman is injecting a sexual culture into the workplace by dressing sexy and provocative, including short skirts and low cut tops, which show her breast, this is obviously intended to draw sexual attention to herself and if she is flirty or dating someone on the job then her behavior is creating a potentially sexually toxic atmosphere and environment for herself and other women.

Why? Because the wearing of "provocative clothes" means she will provoke or entice a man to look at her in a sexual way. In other words, her dressing sexy is clearly intended to draw sexual attention to herself. Therefore, she has no right to complain when a man looks at her in a sexual way. Now, take note that I didn't say a man has a right to say something inappropriate or to touch her.

However, a woman can lure a man into a potentially sexual harassment situation for herself because he will compliment her, by saying things like, "that's a nice sexy dress" or "that dress is hot" or look at her breasts and say "that's a nice top", or look at her legs and say "nice dress" because it's clearly short and sexy. I know what some of you are probably saying. Clothes can't provoke anybody. A man has to control himself. Part of that is true. He has to control himself.

However, the other part is not true. That's the part where "clothes can't provoke anyone." The problem is that the women gets to interpret men's thoughts. She gets to decide his intentions and not him. She gets to determine whether or not that he is complimenting her or harassing her and that's not fair to the man. He should have the opportunity to clarify his statement or comments before she runs off to the Human Resources department to make a sexual harassment claim.

By then it's too late because his reputation is smeared, he gets fired and has his entire life turned upside down and destroyed over her misinterpretation and that's not fair to the man. What do I mean by that? If the woman misinterpreted the conversation and his intent, which in turn makes the woman feel uncomfortable, then that's not his fault, that's her fault,

146

because she should have made him clarify his comment first before she makes a serious sexual harassment claim.

It is clear she has made herself feel that way by her own misinterpretation. Now, some of you maybe be thinking, "but he still made the comment!" Yes, that's true, he did make the comment, but he has every right to voice his opinion. As along as his opinion wasn't sexually harassing. She is the one that misinterpreted his opinion, which caused her to falsely feel and believe that she was sexually harassed. Her misunderstanding is not his fault or problem.

If you still believe that he shouldn't have said anything to her, then you are trying to censor and take away men's voices, and opinions, which we all have and are entitled too. This gives women too much power and control over men when it comes to sexual harassment. We can't allow that to happen. Why? Because that gives the women too much power over men. There's no fairness, balance or room for error. What if she doesn't like him personally or has some kind of grudge or vendetta against him or an axe to grind. Now we have a situation to where the women could weaponizing sex and using it against the man, rather than taking the time to clear up the misunderstanding.

This is how women have clearly weaponized sex, leaving men powerless to defend themselves. That's not fair and that's not right. Why? Because the woman now has all the power and bases all her accusations on the man's opinion, which he is entitled too, and how she "feels" about the situation and not necessarily how it is! It opens up the door for abuse of the justice system and potentially destroys a man's life. All based on a misunderstanding or misinterpreted comment.

The way she dressed created a sexual culture and environment in the workplace. Therefore, the way a woman dresses can provoke sexual thoughts and behavior in men. Why does a woman dress sexy when she goes out to a night club? Because she is trying to draw attention to herself so that guys will give her some attention and possibly approach and talk to her. So why would it be different in the workplace? Only because women are trying to have it both ways.

They want attention from the right person (selective attention). So, if a woman dresses sexy in the club to draw attention, and also dresses sexy in the workplace and draws attention isn't that the same thing? Isn't the goal the same, to draw attention to herself? Sexual attention is sexual attention no matter where you are. I can hear you women now saying, no it's not!

Here's where the confusion comes in and also how the sexual harassment comes into the workplace. Men don't know the difference between why a woman dresses sexy in the club seeking attention and why women dresses sex at work seeking attention. They both look the same to men and this may explain why so many men get caught up with sexual harassment cases.

I know some of you are still saying that that's blaming women. I'm not blaming women for the sexual harassment that they receive through unwanted advances by men in the workplace. Men should control themselves if they know what's best for them. However, what I am doing is I am blaming women for creating a sexually charged atmosphere and environment whenever they are intentionally wearing sexually provocative clothing like short shirts or dresses two inches from their ass that they have to continuously tug at and pull down, because they are too short, and low cut, tight tops showing the top of their breast, and they show up like that to work and expect a man not to be human and keep from being drawn to them.

That's not realistic. I'm saying that you shouldn't intentionally create a sexually charged environment if you don't want unwanted sexual attention. We are not robots or made out of stone. We are all human and that aspect of things has to be taken into consideration. Many women believe that they can do anything that they want to provoke a man and there is nothing he can do about it. That's true, but also irresponsible and dangerous at the same time. It's true that a man shouldn't sexually harass or assault a woman for any reason, but it's also true that it's a very irresponsible and a dangerous thing for a woman to believe that she can dress provocatively and expect no one to say anything, such as compliments or to look at her in the wrong way, such as sexually.

The problem with this irresponsible and dangerous thinking is that she is not accounting for the guy who is interested in her, but she's not interested in him, the nut cases, the crazies and sick people that are out there, who don't understand that they can't do these kind of things, such as sexually harass and assault women. If these men did understand this, then we wouldn't have any sexual assault or harassment cases, now would we?

If a woman draws a man's attention to her sexually, it becomes toxic if she doesn't want that sexual attention from the wrong guy. So, who is the wrong guy? Anyone that she is not attracted too. Which means any or all men that she views as unsuitable to her taste. Someone she will not date.

The problem with this line of thinking is that she can't control who looks at her or who she draws attention from. A woman who dresses sexy in the workplace in order to draw attention to herself, even if she wants targeted attention, (someone she likes) to look at her in a sexual way, she's drawing all eyes on her including unwanted eyes and attention too, and that's where the problem comes in to play. Unwanted attention results in sexual harassment. Now this is a problem in the workplace because no one want sexual harassment on the job. Why? Because men get fired and companies get sued and women get harassed.

The same women who created and injected sexuality into the workplace, by the way they dress, are the same women who are suing for sexual harassment in the workplace. I know some of you are probably saying that it doesn't matter how she dresses; men should just control themselves. The problem with that is that a woman is dressing in that way to "provoke" a sexual reaction to draw attention to herself and that's exactly what she is getting. Attention! It's just not the attention she wants. Meaning, she's getting attention from men she wasn't attracted too.

Some of these women's behavior is subconscious and a lot of it is conscious. However, the outcome is the same. Women wanting and getting sexual attention by the way they dress or behave on the job, and then, destroying or ending someone's career or suing the company when they got negative attention from someone they don't desire. I know some of you are still probably saying that the men should still just control themselves.

That sounds good in theory, however we are all human being with faults and flaws and if a woman is provocative and sexually enticing men on the job by the way she dresses, then she should expect a human response to her enticing or provocative behavior. I'm not saying it's right, only that for every action there is a reaction. In this day and age if a man says the wrong thing or if his words come out wrong then he will be severely punished and charged with sexual harassment, even if he is just complimenting a beautiful sexy woman on the job.

For example, "hey that's a hot dress", "nice legs". That's a compliment coming from a man's point of view, but it could be a viewed as sexual harassment from a woman's point of view. Where's the line and who gets to draw it? Since women are the sexual gatekeepers, they get to make the rules, determine where the lines are and draw the lines themselves, without any input from men. There's no equality or fairness in that for men. That's weaponizing sex.

There are many relationships begin in the workplace or on the job. How does that come about or happen? It means that two people have to be attracted to each other. Right? Which means that a man has to be attracted to a woman and approach her with a sexual intent, because we all know that a woman is not going to approach a man, because they are scared of getting rejected. This can be good for the man or bad for him. He can either get a date, or he can get fired. Therefore, there has to be a balance.

There has to be some kind of fairness for the men, who are just attracted to the woman and want to date her. To me there has to be a default rule in place for men, in order to protect them from misunderstandings, misinterpreted comments or to prevent dishonest vendettas, grudges or women with axes to grind, or their weaponizing sex. The default rule can be something like a two or three strike rule. That's where, if the men have been told by the woman or warned by the company that his behavior is unwanted at least twice, then they can take action against him.

He has to be given a chance to clarify himself or given an opportunity to stop approaching or pursuing a woman who doesn't want to be pursued (because sometimes women won't tell a guy that she is not interested in him and to stop bothering her because she don't want to hurt his feelings). That way he has some power or control over the situation and his job or his future is not all in the woman's hands. This will bring balance and it also keeps the women honest so that they can't use sexual harassment as a dishonest weapon against the men. It also gives the company a chance to warn the men so that they won't get sued by an opportunistic woman, who is looking to enrich herself from a sexual harassment claim that company will have to pay for, but ultimately had nothing to do with.

This could be a possibly solution. If a guy asks a woman out, misinterprets or misunderstands a comment and she rejects him, then he should get at least two strikes before disciplinary action is taken. However, if he asks a different girl out or makes a misinterpreted or misunderstood comment to this different woman, then it should be three strikes before he is out of the company, rather than a one and done.

If the man makes one comment and he is fired, this gives too much power and control to the woman, rather is misunderstood or misinterpreted or not. That way he has been warned by the woman and the company and then he has no excuse for his behavior. Also, the woman gets protected by the company and the company gets to escape from a potential lawsuit from the women. Consequently, women can't weaponize sex in order to gain an unchecked, unchallenged and unbalanced advantage over the men or the company. It's a win-win for everyone. What do you think?

CHAPTER 16

SEXUAL HARASSMENT (A MONEY MOTIVATOR)

Opportunistic Women Who Take Advantage of a Sexual Crisis!

Why do some women sue the employer, who had nothing to do with her harassment, rather than the actual perpetrator who harassed them? It's simple, it's because the company has deep pockets. What I mean is that the employers have plenty enough money to pay for women's pain and suffering. However, the women and women's groups will say, it's because the employer created an unsafe work environment or that they looked the other way and ignored the harassment.

That could possibly be true in some cases, however in the vast majority of cases the employer just doesn't want the publicity and or the negative scrutiny that a sexual harassment case could bring to their company. It's just not worth the trouble, so they settle out of court just to make it go away so they can continue and focus on their business again.

At the same time the women who file these cases also know that the employer will settle the case financially, and there we can find the financial motivations. There are legitimate sexual harassment cases no doubt and these women deserve to be paid for sure, for the bullshit that they had to put up with in the workplace. However, at the same time there are scams, and opportunistic women who are conniving enough to weaponize sex in order to get a large sum pay day, and if there's collateral damage (men) along the way to get to that pay day, then oh well, so be it, too bad for him. That's weaponizing sex.

I know some of you are probably thinking that we have to protect women from sexual abuse from men in the workplace. It can't be tolerated. Yes, I agree with legitimate abuse, but you can't lump all sexual assault or harassment into one basket and paint all claims with a broad brush either, as if they are all one and the same. There has to be a case by case basis analysis. Why? Because there are innocent men swooped up in the emotional outrage that sexual harassment or assault has caused.

A man has to be given due process. Due process is what keeps everyone honest, and everything fair and balanced. We as a society have to make sure that these women are honest and not just trying to get paid or totally destroy someone's (usually men's) life in the process. Why do we have to have honesty, fairness, balance and due process? Because the next time a woman accuses a man of sexual assault it just might be you or someone that you may know or someone close to you, like a male family member. Hmmmm?

I'm quite sure you would want the benefit of the doubt and your American rights to due process. Right? Or is it okay for someone to weaponize sex against you? I guess you will just suffer the consequences, not fight back and allow this person to ruin and destroy your life for their own personal gain? That would be them taking advantage of their being women and that would be weaponizing sex. Why? Because she has gone unchecked, unchallenged and unbalanced.

Why are women sexually enticing men on the job or at their workplace? Women say to men, don't look at them as a sexual object or a piece of meat! But yet many of them display themselves a sexual object or a piece of meat. What do I mean by that? In today's world where women are sexually harassed and sexual assaulted in such a toxic situation in the #MeToo era, women don't want to be sexually harassed but yet why are they sexually enticing men?

Why? Because as long as it's about women getting paid and feeling empowered doing so, then it's okay for women to sexually exploit themselves as long as they benefit from it? This is a major conflict between women and the workplace. Again, I'm not saying that men should or have the right to assault or harass women. However, if a woman intentionally exposes her breasts in order to draw men's attention and have them look at her in a sexual way then she has to take responsibility for creating that situation.

I know some women are probably thinking and saying, "yeah right, that's blaming women" and "the way they dress shouldn't matter!" I'm not blaming women for the harassment or assault that they may have received. But again, I am blaming women for intentionally and sexually enticing men to look at their breasts or body in a sexual way. Then they turn around and say to men, "don't comment, or look at me in a sexual way or it will be viewed as sexual harassment." That thinking defies logic.

The idea that women can instigate the sexual enticement of men and not expect it to lead to sexual harassment or assault is nonsense. I know you are probably thinking, well how are women sexually enticing men on the job or at the workplace? Glad you asked. Here's what I mean by sexually enticing men. Is a restaurant or a bar a place of work for some women? Sure, it is. Then tell me why many women purposely push their breast up and out for a man to look at and be turned on sexually in order to get a better chance in receiving a bigger tip? Why are they intentionally showing men their bodies in a sexual way with the intention to entice them, turn them on, but with zero desire of having sexual relations with them?

In other words, are they creating a sexual environment and purposely teasing the men sexually, displaying themselves to men like a piece of meat and a sexual object just to get a tip from them? Also these women understand that the more skin they show, the more sexy they look, the more a man will be sexually attracted to them and that sexual tease and turn on will make the men spend more money and therefore the women will get a bigger tip.

That's the insidious plan behind the sexual game that these women on the job and at the workplace are playing. But let one of the guys call them on their bluff for sexual enticing them, then watch it quickly become a sexual harassment or potential assault claim if the man says something or touches them inappropriately. The men don't have the right to harass or touch without permission, but it's the women who are playing this sexual game with the men. It's the women who are injected the idea of sex into the workplace. It's the women who intentionally sexually enticing the men. It's the women who have created a sexual environment by dressing as sexy as they can in order to sexually tease a man into giving her a bigger tip.

So why aren't the women taking accountability and responsibility for creating a dangerous sexual harassment environment for themselves on the job? This is a conflict within the women. Not the men. Women have to take accountability for their part in the lead up to the sexual harassment situation. I say lead up because there is always smoke before there is fire.

Women who prepare and groom themselves for sexually attention by wearing tight bras that push their breast up and out of their tops and put on short skirts and dresses that barely cover the bottom of their asses are purposely drawing men attention to those sexual areas in order to get them sexually aroused so that the men will be interested in them, then the women can use sex to manipulate the men out of their money.

Here's a tip. Don't say it's all the man's fault no matter what, when it's clear that it is the women that are sexually enticing men, intentionally and purposely injecting a sexual atmosphere into the entire situation. Women intentionally dress sexy on the job, then they want men to be a robot and not look at them in a sexual way. Men are naturally attracted to sexy women. Hello?

Men are human and the natural thing for a man to do is to look at and be attracted to a pretty, sexy woman. That's his natural instinct. Therefore, that's what he is going to do, and these women know this and that's why they dress sexy in order to attract the men's attention to them sexually. Why? Because sex sells and, in this case, women are advertising and selling themselves for higher tips, wages or promotions. Women want it both ways.

They want men's sexual attention when it financially benefits them, but they don't want to take responsibility for the negative consequences that comes with sexually enticing men. That's them taking advantage of their being women. Reaping all the positive benefits (such as money) but accepting no accountability or blame for the negative aspects of their starting the fire, which drew the interests of the potential harasser to her sexually, even though it is the women who are the ones who orchestrated the entire sexual situation.

For the women who created the entire sexual environment and atmosphere, there is a very good chance that sexual harassment or assault doesn't happen, such as in the cases where women intentionally provoke a sexual response and attention from men by dressing sexy in order to attract and entice those men. Therefore, women can't have it both ways. You can't complain that there's a sexual harassment or an assault problem in today's society and then turn around and intentionally sexually entice men for financial gain in the workplace or on the job. You must choose one side or the other.

CHAPTER 17

WHY WOMEN SHOULDN'T HAVE MULTIPLE SEX PARTNERS AT ONE TIME

It's Her Body and Her Choice—to Damage and Destroy it if She wants!

Should women have multiple sex partners at one time?

According to the average man the answer is NO! Why not?

Because today's women are more unfaithful now than ever. Why? Because the feminists and the women's groups have brainwashed women into believing that they can do anything that a man can do, and that includes having more than one sexual partner at a time. Why are they encouraging women to basically be whores in the eyes of most men?

The reason why men use the word "whores" and not referring to them as having sex like a man is because women are all about respect. They want total respect from men. You always hear the phrase "respect for women" thrown around like it's one of the Ten Commandments for women. Holier-than-thou. Therefore, if women want the utmost respect from men, then why are they running around acting like prostitutes in heat? Or "whores" in men's eyes?

Men say they use the word "whores" because women should have more self-respect for their bodies and their reputations. Many of today's women don't even know who's the father(s) of their baby(ies). That's sad, and I feel bad for the child. However, women are following in the negatives of their male counterparts. Many of them feel like if a man can cheat then so should they. They say, "what's wrong with that?" Plenty.

Women—-Men and women are not the same, we are not equal in everything, no matter what you've been told. How so? Because the biggest differences with a man and a woman are the consequences for the negative actions that they take. If a man cheats on his girlfriend or wife and she finds out, then she will most definitely be angry at him or she may leave him.

The biggest mistake that he can make is to have a baby with another girl while he is with his girlfriend or wife and that would be extremely bad for everyone, including the baby. However, he can still continue on with his lifestyle without upsetting his daily routine. He may have to pay child support, but he doesn't have to raise the child himself. That responsibility would be on the woman, whom he got pregnant, unfortunately for her.

Why? Because she has to raise that child if she doesn't get an abortion. However, if a woman cheats then she becomes a single mother and the problems begin. There are major life consequences for her negative actions. A woman's entire life is turned upside down if she decides to keep the child. Her entire future will be altered.

She can't be free to go to school like she used to because she has a baby to take care of. It will be hard to find a babysitter or childcare. She will need more money now because she has another mouth to feed. She will have a hard time dating men because many of them don't want to deal with a single mother and babies' fathers and the problems and baggage that comes along with that situation. She will have a host of issues and problems that a man just wouldn't have under the same circumstances.

Therefore, men and women are not equal! Women have to adjust their mentality and attitudes when it comes to sex, and account for the negative consequences of cheating and having casual sex that men don't need to.

Chapter 18

MAN CODES: THE DIRTY LITTLE SECRETS ABOUT SEX THAT MEN DON'T TELL WOMEN!

What's a man code?

A man code is the raw beliefs that men keep to themselves and never tell women how they really feel about them. Why? Because men believe that women can't handle the truth about what's really in their minds when it comes to sex.

"Man code"

Why do men call women "whores" or "hoes?"

Is it because they are just upset and angry at the women?

No. Men call women "whores" or believe that they are "whores" because women will not have sex with men unless they either gives them money, pays for the date, buy them gifts, or some other form of gift through trips or entertainment, which all cost men money, all in exchange for having sex with a them. Most women will demand or require this. To most men it's no different from prostitution.

What's a prostitute? A "whore", right? A woman who demands money for sex. Which is a *whore*. However, men will not tell a woman that to her face because he doesn't want to hurt her feelings. So, he only says this when he is mad at her. At that point he doesn't care if he hurts her feelings or not. The bottom line is that the majority of women make men pay some kind of monetary price to have sex with them.

Why? Because women are the sexual gatekeepers and they get to determine what having sex with them is worth to the man. I've heard some mothers tell their daughters to not have sex for free. The mothers say to the daughter, "if you are going to have sex you may as well get paid for it". That's the definition of a *whore* to many men. A rose is still a rose by any other name and sex for money is sex for money under any other name. A dirty little secret about men's thoughts that men don't tell women.

"Man code"

What do men really think about women having multiple sex partners at one time? One of the "dirty" little secrets that men don't tell women is that they believe that having sex with

165

a woman with a large, stretched and worn out vagina is not enjoyable or desirable because she has had sex with too many men and multiple sex partners at one a time. They compare it to having sex with a bucket of water. Men will never tell a woman this because he doesn't want to hurt her feelings. Men believe that women can't handle the truth that her body is undesirable to the point that no man will want her sexually.

If a woman has multiple sex partners at the same time, most men won't feel like the sex with her would be enjoyable. Why not? Because we all know that a vagina stretches to fit the biggest penis. Men say that if a woman's vagina is not tight then they really don't want her sexually, because it's no longer enjoyable or desirable. If you know what I mean.

I know some of you women are saying, "so what" or "it shouldn't matter." However, it does matter to a man who wants to be in a long-term relationship with you. Women—If a man doesn't enjoy having sex with you, then he will look for sex with another woman, maybe someone with less "miles" on her. Meaning a woman who hasn't been stretched or worn out because of all the multiple penises that she has had in her lifetime.

Now that may sound graphic or not true to you, but to men it's true and a factor to them staying with a woman long term. Believe it or not! He may tolerate you but will probably wind up cheating on you with another woman with a more enjoyable vagina. Women—have you ever seen a man cheat on a pretty woman with a less attractive woman? I'm telling you that part of the reason for that is because he didn't enjoy the sex with the pretty woman because of her lager oversized vagina.

Many women believe that men are just dogs and looking for any woman who will have sex with them. That's not the case. Think about it. A man will stay with an unattractive woman as long as she has a tight, enjoyable vagina who can give good sex. That's a serious secret that men won't tell women.

It's like a woman who is with a man with a small penis. She really doesn't want to be stuck with him for the rest of her life having bad sex. So, she shops around. Unfortunately, during her man shopping quest, she is being stretched open and worn out and making herself not desirable to other men who may want to be in a serious relationship with her because of it. Believe it or not! Men will tolerate women with whom they don't enjoy sex with, even if they have a large vagina; however, it will go from being desirable and satisfying to just something to do.

He is thinking— "let me hurry up and finish" because he really can't feel anything, meaning her vagina walls. To men it's like have sex with a bucket of water. I know a lot of women will think that the man is just small, but have you ever thought that maybe your vagina is just large? Some women get their vagina tightened so that she and her man can both enjoy sex. Believe it or not!

Now I know some women are probably saying, "why are you talking about women in that way?" Because these are things that men won't tell you. Don't believe it? Ask a man why is one of his fantasies is to have sex with a virgin? You may be thinking it's because he will be her first. That's a small part of it but the bigger part is that, it's because her vagina is very tight and it's going to be very enjoyable because she hasn't been stretched open to the point that he can't feel her and it's not enjoyable to him.

Women— let me let you in on a little secret that men keep to themselves. Men like women with tight vaginas. They don't like having sex with a woman with a large vagina because all he can think about is number of penises that's been there before him. To him, that woman is damaged goods. If you don't believe this explain why when men get older, they go look for a younger woman? You may be thinking that it's because they want to control her or that the men have control issues right?

That's a small part of it but the bigger part is that they believe that a younger woman will have a tighter vagina and that the sex will be more desirable to him. Believe or not! Women—have you ever wondered why a man only lasts two minutes in the bed while having sex? It's not all because he has a premature ejaculation problem. It's because the woman doesn't have a tight vagina and it's not good to him, so he just wants to hurry up and get out of there. Believe or not!

Women—this is a secret that a man won't tell you. A man won't tell you those things because he doesn't won't to hurt your feelings and he wants to keep having sex with you even if your vagina does not feel that good to him. But it's temporary. He will be looking to find another woman with a tighter vagina in the future. But he won't let you go until he has another one. Believe it or not!

Women, that's one of the main reasons why men cheat on you. It's because the sex is not good, and that's because the woman's vagina is not tight and he is thinking that maybe you had to many large penises from too many different guys and that your vagina didn't snap back into place. That's damaged goods to him. Believe it or not!

But he won't tell you that. He will lie about it before he will hurt your feelings. However, this is the reason women shouldn't cheat or have multiple sexual partners, because the vagina stretches and sometimes it doesn't snap back into place and that's what's on a man's mind when he finds out you've been with multiple guys at a time. Believe or not.

You maybe being saying to yourself, "well he can go to hell! If he doesn't want it then some man will." And that's probably true. But I'm telling you this is how most men feel. Therefore, you will run across the same thing down the road. So, don't listen to the feminists and let them tell you to have multiple sex partners at one time because it will ruin your body in the eyes of a man. Believe it or not!

"Man Code"

Oral sex—Women

Women— have you ever wondered why a man won't go down on you? Well let me tell you the real reason why he won't go down and give you oral sex. If you are just casually dating a man, he sees you as someone who is dating other guys too. Therefore he thinks or believes that you are having sex with multiple guys, so he thinks that you are unclean and may have just had sex recently with one of those other guys and he may just eat the other guy's ejaculation.

I know that's sounds disgusting and gross but that's what he thinks, so he will not even entertain the thought. That's the real reason why he won't give you oral sex. You may be thinking that that's crazy because you wash your vagina. It doesn't matter what you believe, it's what *he* believes and along with many other men. Women who casually date or cheat and sleep around, this is the view and opinion of you by men.

They see you as a whore with no self-respect. However, this is a secret that they won't tell you because they feel as long as you are easy to have sex with, they will get free sex with no strings attached. They see it this way. Why take you out and wine and dine you, why spend any money on you when they can get the sex at no cost? Pleasing you is not in their long-term plans. You are just not worth it to them. So, they put you in rotation with other girls as just a piece of ass to have sex with when they have a slow night. But they are not going to tell you that.

Women—word of advice: don't ever let a man know that you are casually dating. Why? Because he will automatically put you in the "Hoe Zone". What's a "Hoe Zone"? A *Hoe Zone* is when a man finds out that a woman is cheating, casually dating, or not interested in a relationship, and he immediately puts her there as someone to just have sex with. It's the opposite of a woman who puts a man in the "Friend Zone", as someone she is not going to have sexual relationships with. However, a man will not tell a woman this secret.

Why? Because to men, these women don't have any self-respect therefore they don't have any self-worth, so men just use them as their personal whores. The men never have any intentions of getting into a serious relationship with these women because they see them a someone that they can't trust. They believe these women have no morals and will one day cheat on them, so this is men's way of getting at the women before the women get at them. This is a man code secret that men will never tell women.

"Man Code"

Oral Sex —Men

Another dirty little secret that men have about sex that men won't tell women is that they prefer oral sex over vaginal sex. Why? Because a woman's mouth is tighter than her vagina. It feels a lot better because he feels that her vagina is wore out and don't have the right wetness and tightness that he likes. He feels as if he can get her to give him oral sex, A.K.A. a blow job, that that would satisfy him better than her vagina, which he is tired of, because he can't enjoy it anymore because it just doesn't feel good to him anymore.

This is why many men cheat on women and want a different woman's vagina because he feels that it would bring back excitement to him so he can enjoy sex again. However, he will not tell this to his woman because that would hurt her feelings and tear down her self-esteem. He doesn't want to leave her, but he doesn't know how to say, "give me a blow job because it feels better than your vagina." So, he keeps this dirty little secret to himself. He'd rather cheat on her than to tell her that.

At the same time, he believes that if she gives him oral sex, (which many women stop doing when they get into a long-term relationship) then he wouldn't cheat on her. I know it sounds crazy but it true. Believe it or not! So, women word of advice. Give your man more oral sex and he won't cheat on you. Why? Because a woman who can give good oral sex is priceless to a man, because she is hard to find. Therefore, he won't want to lose her, and he will appreciate her more than a woman who just give him regular, routine sex. This is a dirty little secret that men keep to themselves about sex and won't tell women. Believe it or not.

CHAPTER 19

WHY CAN'T TODAY'S WOMEN BE TRUSTED IN A RELATIONSHIP?

Why do Women Cheat More Than Men In Today's Society?

Because they have sexual abundance and sex comes to women a dime a dozen therefore women can get upset at men for any reason and they can give away sex to random men in an instant and nine out of ten men will accept the sexual gift from even an average woman.

Women cheat on their boyfriends or husbands because they can. I know some of you will say it's because she's not getting enough emotional support, or he was not treating her right and so on. Blah blah blah. Those are some of the many excuses that women give men when they cheat on them. But it all comes down to the fact that they do it because they can.

Women are the sexual gatekeepers. All sexual activity goes through them. So, they get to decide if and when sex happens. They make the choices of who to have sex with and where to have it. And last but not least, they determine for themselves the reason why they are cheating in the first place. Therefore, they can make up any excuse or reason that they want. Women cheat because they can.

Women have sexual abundance. This means they can have sex with as many men as they want because it's easy for women to have sex because most men are willing partners. All pretty women or even average women have to do is say, "let's have sex" to a man, and 99.999% of the time, men will do it. So, sex comes a dime a dozen to women. Women cheat because they are no better than the men who cheat. As a matter of fact, they are one and the same. Women and men who do so are both no good, deceitful, scum, dirty and deserve many other narcissistic names that you can call them.

Women have proven that they can be just as nasty as men can be. I know you are probably saying "why are you so hard on a woman when she cheats but not on men when they cheat?" The reason why I say these women are like men and are no good cheaters is because, they could have just left the men if they didn't like them. They simply could have broken up and ended the relationship. However, they didn't! They choose to stay in the relationship and do all kind of sick, twisted, dirty and disgusting things behind his back. They choose to cheat with other men and share with them the same body parts that they share with their partners.

To leave their boyfriend or husband and go behind his

back with some strange man to have sex with him in her same space (vagina) and possibly mixing body fluids and giving this strange man oral sex and then coming back home to kiss her boyfriend or husband in the mouth is just disgusting. You're probably thinking, that's a harsh thing to say about a woman. It's graphic and disrespectful and is disgusting language. That's because what they are doing is graphic disrespectful and disgusting.

I know the next question will be—what about the men? If you read the topic again, then you will see that it says, "why do women cheat." Not men.

Now—this may just be harsh talk to some people. However, that's not the point. The point is—is it true? And is it's true that's that a possibility? If the answer is "yes", then so be it. Sometimes the truth hurts. Sometimes you have to put the raw truth out there, and not sugar coat it in order to get people to think about their actions. You have to let them see what they are really doing to another person, and how that person has been affected and how they view or see them now. Now maybe they can understand why this person is so angry and upset at their disrespectful and disgusting ways. Maybe next time they'll think about their actions—-when the next person cheats on them. Hmmmm? Karma's a bitch!

Chapter 20

SEXUAL ABUNDANCE VS SEXUAL SCARCITY

Why do Women have Abundance and Men have Scarcity?
Which Leads to Many Men Cheating!

Women have the abundance because they are the sexual gatekeepers. They get to pick and choose when, where and with whom to have sex with. They make the rules and draw the lines to all sexual activity. Why? Because it's their bodies and they get to determine if sex takes place or not. Men have scarcity because they have to wait for the women's approval and consent before they can have sex.

Being the sexual gatekeepers and having abundance is a double-edged sword. Why? You would think that it would be a good thing for women, right? You would think that women would enjoy all that power and control over sex? Well there is a negative side to having sexual abundance. Having sexual abundance also means sexual boredom. A woman can and will get tired of sex. She will become less exited, no enthusiasm more complacent about sex.

Having the abundance of sex is like a having brand-new car. You start out loving it and can't wait to drive it and show it off to friends and family. However, after three or four years it starts to get old, and you start to notice all the dings and dents. It's not as clean as it once was when it was new. It doesn't perform and drive as smooth as it used to. And now you are looking to trade it in for something new.

Women having the abundance of sex, meaning they can have sex anytime they want, is just like that new car. Women get bored with it. It's not as exciting as it used to be, and they don't have that energy anymore. They don't look forward to having sex anymore. The men don't perform like they used to, and now they view it as overrated and now they don't want to have sex unless they have to. They'd rather masturbate.

So, then they slow down the sex with their partners or don't want to have sex with them at all, eventually. Now where does that leave the man in this situation? S.O.L., meaning "shit out of luck". Now he is frustrated because he doesn't know what's going on with his partner and why she doesn't want to have sex with him like she used too. He starts thinking that there is something wrong with him. Then he starts to think that maybe she is having an affair. Then he just gives up trying to understand her and then he may start to have his own affair because of lack of sex from her. Many women in relationships come across this negative abundance phase. Many of them are completely unaware that the abundance phase exists. Here is an example of what negative abundance does to a woman and her relationship.

I talked to a woman and she told me that she and her husband had been married for 5 years and that they barely have sex anymore, and she told me that they were both just so busy that they don't have time for it or they are just so tired and exhausted and don't have the energy it takes for sex. I asked her how many hours a day did both of them work. She said they worked eight hour shifts and they are off on the weekends. I said that's routine and nothing strenuous. I didn't see this hectic schedule that she claimed she had. So, I asked her when did the lack of sex begin. She said about year two of their marriage.

I asked, "how do you know that time frame? What made you aware of that date or around that date?" She said, it's because "that's when I didn't have a job and all we did was have sex and I just got tired and bored." I asked, "did you get bored with sex because of sex or just got bored from not working and doing nothing all day?" She said both.

She said when he was around all she did was masturbate and then that got old, tired and boring. She said that now she just has no interest because she can have sex any time she wants and there's no excitement or fun in that. I said, "oh that's it. It's not that you don't have time because it seems like you have plenty of time to have sex. It's because you have that abundance, and you can have sex at any time you want to, and you are just making excuses for yourself." She said, "I'm making excuses because I don't want to tell him that I'm bored with sex since it's overrated to me now." I said, "well what about him? Doesn't he want to have sex with you?" She said, "yeah, but I just make excuses about being tired so he won't bother me."

I said, "why don't you have sex with him anyway just to satisfy him?" She said, "I'm really not interested if he is satisfied or not, he can take care of himself (masturbate)." She said, "it's my body and I could have sex anytime I want to with him, if I chose, so I'm fine, he's the one with the problem not me." I said, "so you don't care as long as you have the abundance." She said, "yeah pretty much". Then she said, "I think he's probably cheating on me anyway since I'm not giving him sex."

Now I am telling you this story so that you can see and understand that women have a "sexually abundance" mindset, and how it can backfire against them. Her marriage is not going to last, and she knows it. "Okay," you may be asking, "what are women supposed to do about it?" This is simple. Sometimes women have to sacrifice and satisfy their partners from time to time, even if they don't want to.

Oh, I know some of you women are probably saying that a woman shouldn't have to have sex if she doesn't want to. It's her body and no man can tell her what to do with her body. Yes, that's right, no man can make her do anything she doesn't want to, and no one is implying or forcing her to have sex against her will. However, what I am saying is that she should sacrifice for her partner from time to time.

Women can't be so selfish to the point where they completely shut their partners out of sex, and still want him to remain in a relationship with them. Sex is very important to men and if they don't get it from their female partners then they will get it from another female somewhere. You may be saying that men shouldn't cheat on a woman no matter what. That sounds good in theory, but you can be sure if he knew that he was signing up for a sexless marriage or relationship he wouldn't go through with it at all! So, she needs to hold up her obligation in the relationship and that includes sex! But if she doesn't want to have sex because it's her body then that's her right. But don't expect a man to hold up his end either and be faithful to her. That street goes both ways. There's a price to pay!

CHAPTER 21

THE CONSEQUENCES OF ONE NIGHT STANDS AND CASUAL SEX

From Single Mothers to Murdering (Abortion) Mothers and STD's for Fun!

Let's talk about casual sex for women and men.

Why do men and women want to have casual sex? The answer is clear, and that's because neither one of them wants a long-term commitment or relationship. Why not? Probably because some of them have been hurt in past relationships or maybe they are just too busy with their job or work for a relationship but they still want to have sex with somebody or maybe they can't find the right person so they just settle for sex only. There are multiple reasons why people have casual sex. So how did we get to this point in society where casual sex is okay?

Men have been trying to have sex with women since the beginning of time but women who are the moral sexual gatekeepers have stopped men from having casual with them and have kept them in check regarding sex. What do I mean when I say, "kept them in check?" Women in past generations have had a very high moral standing with themselves and their God. Women use to make men wait until marriage before they had sex with a man. They wouldn't live in with a man either, A.K.A. "shack up" with him.

Women have made men commit to them by withholding sex from men until they complied to the woman's strong values about her body. Women had very high self-respect and wouldn't allow men to turn them into whores by having sex before they got married. Men had no choice but to comply and respect her values. Which meant that less babies were born out of wedlock and became bastard children.

Men have always been the instigator for casual sex; however, women wouldn't allow the men to get out of control and they gave more respect for themselves and their bodies. Women saw their bodies as a temple because they knew that they were the sexual gatekeepers and had to control and tame the men's animalistic behaviors. Women had men and their sexual tendencies under control until feminists group brainwashed and told them that they can have sex just like a man, and why not?

If men can have casual sex, then so can women. "Let's make everything equal" is what they told women. Even in sex. Well, there is a few things wrong with the word "equal". Men and women are not equal when it comes to sex because, first, women want to be respected by men. It's at the top of their list or maybe the number one thing that women want from men. Therefore, if a woman goes and behaves like a man, by having sex with random partners like men do, then whoops, there goes the respect right out of the window. Why is the respect gone? Because a woman has lost her self-respect and her value or worth to a man has totally diminished.

Why? Because the more she has casual sex with multiple men the more men will view her as a *whore*. And we all know that a man will not take a *whore* home to meet his mother. Also, there is a phycological effect that most men can't get past after they find out about a woman's past sexual history, after she admits to having had casual sex or multiple one-night stands. Believe it not. But these are some of the things that go through their minds. Many men have to try and un-ring the bell that is going off in their heads about a woman who has had multiple sex partners.

Bad images flash in their heads and in the back of their minds about a woman having had sex with multiple, random men. Warning, this may be a little graphic but it's true. A man may also be wondering how he measures up with the other guys, like is his penis big enough for her after she has had so many men? Is she tight enough now that so many different sized penises have stretched her vagina out? Is she thinking about one of the other guys she's had sex with while she is having sex with him? Is she clean enough after having all those different penises come inside of her? Can he even satisfy her? Is she damaged goods now? Is she tired and bored of sex and just not that interested in it anymore after she's had so many men? And so on.

These are some of the things that go through many men's minds when they find out about a woman's past sexual history. Believe or not! Women—a word of advice. Never tell a man that you're interested in or in a relationship with about your past sexual history. I know you are probably thinking, "why not? I want to be honest with him."

Trust me, he really doesn't want to know how many men have handled you. Warning! If you decide to go through and tell him anyways, expect him to view you differently after you let him know. He may not say anything about it, or he may brush it off in front of you, however he will think of you differently and have sex with you differently too. Trust me. Keep some things to yourself. You will be a lot better off if he didn't know.

All things are not created equal. Believe it or not, no matter what you've been told. It's quite the opposite.

Secondly, and it's a huge deal. Women can get pregnant and have babies, so if a woman goes and acts like a man does and have multiple sex partners then she puts herself at risk, not only for STD's, but having a baby without a father and then becoming a single mother and all the stress and pressure that comes with that situation.

Now you may be saying to yourself, "but a man did this to her, he got her pregnant, so why isn't he part responsible for this situation?" The answer is—he is part responsible if she knows his real name, where he lives, social security number, etc. See the problem with women having casual sex and one-night stands is that, they are at far more risk than a man, because of the burden of them getting pregnant. Men can't get pregnant.

You say, "but they get the women pregnant?" Yes, that's true but men don't have to carry a baby inside of their bodies for nine long months. But women do! Men don't have to raise that child. But women do! Men don't have to put their careers on hold. But women do! Men don't have change their lives to fit the child's needs. But women do. Men don't have to alter their entire future for the child. But women do. Men don't have to have a gruesome abortion if it's not in their best interests. But women do. And so on.

There's a lot at stake and a lot of life changing challenges for women when they go out and act like a man and have casual sex or one-night stands with a guy that they don't even know. Challenges that men don't have. But women do! So, when the feminists tell women to go out and have sex like men because men and women are equal, they lie to women because as you can see now that there is nothing equal between men and women having casual sex or one-night stands. Women have more serious consequences to face for their actions in that matter that men just don't have.

If women continue to behave like men and have casual sex and one-night stands (with guys they don't even know) then they must suffer the consequences of their actions and it's nobody's fault but theirs, and theirs alone; because they are in control and totally responsible for all bad or negative behavior. Not men! Because they are the sexual gatekeepers. As far as men's part or consequences for their actions, if they get a woman pregnant, we all know consequence of their behavior, and that is child support! So, men——There's still a price to pay!

Third, Safety. Safety for women is another top priority for them. I've seen many women who have put their personal safety in jeopardy in the name of equality. Here's what I mean. I've seen women go to the bar or night club and go home with a guy for a one-night stand because they figured if men can do them why not women? Now that sounds good and sounds logically equal for women. However, they are missing one key component in all of this equality talk, and that's safety. Man can take a woman home with him for a one-night stand and 99.999% of the time doesn't have to worry about his personal safety because in many cases he is bigger and stronger than the woman and he can handle himself physically.

I know there are some women that are saying that women can be just as tough as men and can handle themselves too. Okay that may right in some instances, because there are exceptions to every rule. However, the rules say differently. Now, who are the majority of victims of rape, sexual assault or murder from a one-night stand? Women! So let's keep it real! Therefore, women have to be more concerned about their safety then men as a rule, not an exception.

If women have to be more careful in certain situations because their lives may be in danger, then why do women go home or a hotel or wherever to have a one-night stand? Because the call to be equal by feminists and women's groups and not look weak to a man has caused women to put the concept of equality over their safety and that's just not smart.

Women who are trying to prove a point in being equal to

men in every way including sexually put themselves at high risk and borderlines on stupidity if they put their safety in jeopardy to do it. Women—Again everything is not equal between men and women no matter what you've been told! However, women are the sexual gatekeepers; it's their bodies and they can do whatever they want with them, including risking their safety and lives to prove a point.

Here's an example of what I mean: I talked to a woman who will remain nameless at this time. She told me that she met a guy at the club and they both were a little tipsy from drinking and dancing. She was with her girlfriends, but she was really interested in this guy that she met. They had a very good time and he seemed like a nice guy. He had asked her back to his place for a "night cap". *Night cap* is code word for let's have sex! Anyway, she should have known that he was full of shit when he used the phrase "night cap". Who in the hell uses the words "night cap" anymore? Cavemen I guess, because that phrase is old as hell.

Anyway, she told her girlfriends that she was going to go home with this guy that she had just met. Her friends tried to warn her, but she didn't listen because she really liked the guy and wanted to have sex with him. So, they caught a cab and went back to his place. When they got there, she had noticed that he had three other male roommates. He told her not to pay any attention to them and the proceeded to his room.

While in his room she began to take off her clothes and get in bed. The guy had gone to use the bathroom. While he was in the bathroom the three roommates had come into the room and told her, while she was laying in the bed naked, that they are into the "share program". She said what is the "share program" they said, "we share all of our women." In other words, they all get to have sex with her. She started to yell for the guy to come in the room and kick them out. The guy said to her that it was okay for her to have sex with them too. She said, "what the hell do you mean I'm not having sex with those guys" he said to her, "yes you are you little slut, you ain't nothing but a whore anyway."

So, she went to get up and leave but she was naked, and she didn't want those guys to see her naked, so she stayed in the bed and told them to leave the room. She started to yell and scream and threatened to call the police. So, the guys told her to go ahead because they just wanted to see her naked once she got up from the bed. She said that she had got up and start to put on her clothes when one of the guys had grabbed her arm and snatch her clothes out of her hand. She then started to scream and yell and cry.

They guys then told her that they thought that she was willing to have sex with them because she came over to a stranger's house alone, so they thought that she was a freak and a whore. She said that one of the guys said to her, "what kind of a stupid bitch are you to come to a guy house that you don't know" and at that point they told her to get out of their house.

So, she put on her clothes and left. She told me that she was scared that they all would rape her, but they didn't. She said that she felt lucky and that she would never do that again. The reason why I tell this story is because women have been given a false sense of hope that everything for them will be equal, but they don't take into account many of the nutcases that are out there.

Many women are so busy trying to prove a point to be equal to men in every way, including sexually, that they throw their common sense and logic out of the window and are willing to put their safety in jeopardy to prove a worthless point! This story just goes to show women that everything is not fair and equal. Look out for your safety first, because a one-night stand is not the same or equal to man when sex is involved. To those women who still want to prove a point that you're sexually equal to a man and put your safety on the line— good luck.

CHAPTER 22

SEXUAL ASSAULT

Sexual assault is the forcing and unwanted touching of a woman against her will and or her consent. This is the only time that women as the sexual gatekeepers are not in charge of sexual activities. Sexual assault is a very serious, disturbing and terrifying thing that many women have gone through and should not be tolerated under any circumstances. However, what if a woman falsely accused a man of sexual assault, what if the consequences or punishment for her lies?

We all know the consequences for a man. He will lose his job, be publicly shamed and embarrassed and go to jail. But what if he didn't actually commit the assault and the woman lies for whatever reason. What should her punishment be for trying to ruin and totally destroyed this man family and his life? Rarely, if at all do the women get punishment for this despicable behavior of falsely accusing a man of sexual assault or rape.

A woman can accuse a man of sexual assault without any evidence, and then society and the media will try to make him prove that he didn't commit the crime. This is as backwards as can be because according to the law a person is presumed innocent until proven guilty, not the other way around. What happens is that a woman will accuse a man of sexual assault then the media will block out the woman's face so that no one can identify her and then proceed to call her a victim, without any proof whatsoever.

What this does is places the man on the defensive again, without any proof that he committed a crime, by plastering the man's picture all of the news and hiding the woman's face it automatically draws the conclusion that his is guilty of the crime. This is highly prejudicial and inflammatory against the man. Once a jury is picked out for this sexual assault case, they would already be coming from the standpoint that he is guilty, because of the negativity that it draws. Now, what if after a grueling trial evidence is found to exonerate him, then what happens to the woman accuser? I'll tell you what happens to her, and that is absolutely nothing.

Why not? Because the women's activist groups will say that because some other men have committed sexual assault, punishing a false accuser would discourage other women from coming forward, of which they have no data or evidence to back this up. Therefore, the woman will usually get off scot-free. This is wrong and there should be some kind of punishment or consequence for her false allegation and lies. Otherwise this will encourage other women to falsely accuse men because they know that there will be no punishment for their actions.

Now it's amazing that women and women's groups believe that punishing the woman will discourage other women from coming forward and reporting their cases. Yet at the same time they don't believe that a false accusation will encourage other false accusations from being made. That means that it's a lose-lose for men and a win-win for women. This is weaponizing sex! This is an example of women being unchecked, unchallenged and it makes things unbalanced between men and women! This is taking advantage of being a woman!

We have to have fairness in our society, because remember ladies, if we don't have fairness then we don't have equality, which most women preach. So, practice what you preach otherwise one day this will be your husband, or boyfriend or even your son. How would you feel then? I'm quite sure if the shoe was on the other foot you will sound just like the men who are screaming for fairness.

CHAPTER 23

SEXUAL HARASSMENT

Women Dictate the Rules, Draw the Lines and Determine
men's rights, Leaving Him Defenseless

Sexual harassment is a different issue because there is a
major problem with the definition of "harassment". The
definition of sexual harassment has a very gray area and is
interpreted only by the women who are making the claim and
often regardless of the intent of the man being accused. The
definition is not clear and is probably one of the reasons why
so many men cross the line and are accused of it.

It is very easy for a man to cross the line of sexual
harassment because it is usually based on how the women
"feel" about the situation. That is a very low bar and standard.
There are checks and balances in almost every situation and
there should be a check and balance for accusers also. Because
if there's no checks or balances on behalf of men, then who's

going to keep the women honest? Who's going to protect the men's rights if they falsely accused?

If we as a society are going to just believe the women first, then that means the men have to prove their innocence and that's not how due process works in this country. All women are not liars, but all women are not honest either and that's why we need checks and balances to keep everything fair on both sides. This is what's so frustrating for men who don't have bad intentions but have been seen as crossing the line in some women's eyes. What do I mean by this?

Well, here's an example for you. I've talked to thousands of men and women. I had a conversation with a guy, and he had told me that he had asked a woman out on a date at his job and she told him that she would "let him know". Well, he saw her a couple of more days that week, he just spoke to her briefly and kept going about his business, and he had no further conversations with her. The following week when he came in to work the manager, his boss and called him into the office to talk to him.

The manager had told him that he was being accused of sexual harassment from a coworker. He said, "I didn't harass anyone." The manager told him who had made the claim and why she made the claim. He was in shock because it was the woman that he had asked out on a date. She had told the manager that she felt very uncomfortable around him and that he would stare and look at her in a strange way. Then she told the manager that he was harassing her by continuously asking her out on a date.

The guy said that he had only asked her out one time and

that he was waiting on her response. The manager told him that he had to suspend him until further notice. The guy was very upset that he could lose his job and become homeless if he couldn't pay his rent. Well, the following week the manager called him and gave him the bad news that he was fired. The guy asked the manager why he was firing him. The manager told him that it was confirmed that he did ask the accuser out on a date and that's what was considered harassment in her eyes because she felt uncomfortable.

The guy said to the manager that he had only asked her out once. The manager said that once is enough if she "feels" uncomfortable. The way that woman "felt" is all that mattered, is what the manager had told him, and just like that it was all over, and he got fired. This story stuck in my head because I was stunned that a man could get fired for sexual harassment after merely asking a woman out on a date with no bad intentions.

He got no due process; the entire decision was based on how she "felt" and not his intent. This man's life got ruined simply for asking the wrong woman out on a date. This is a very dangerous precedent for women when they are given all the power in sexual harassment cases and where everything is based on how they "feel". Women are very emotional and on any given day those emotions can swing one way or the other and that's not fair for men. There has to be a standard put in place in order to keep things fair and balanced for men as well. Otherwise their future livelihoods will be at stake.

The ability to feed and take of themselves will be in jeopardy all because they said the wrong thing to the wrong woman. I know what some of you are thinking. You're probably thinking that he should have been more careful about what he said, and this wouldn't have happened to him. Or that somehow maybe he deserved it. However way you look at it, I don't think that he should have been fired just for asking her out one time. I thought harassment was a repeated thing. Something that has to happen over and over again, right?

However if women get to draw the line of sexual harassment based on how they "feel" then men are in big trouble in this country because how she "feels" can lead to abuse of power, and that wouldn't be a country that many people want to live in. Why would it lead to abuse? You're probably thinking. Because what if a woman just doesn't like the guy or has something against him like maybe they are going for the same promotion and he is her top competition.

She can just easily say that he harassed her and down he goes. Or maybe they dated at one time and now it has gone sour, she can then turn around and say that he makes her "feel" uncomfortable, and she charges him with sexual harassment and he can't defend himself because he has no real due process. This is a very dangerous, slippery slope for society with regards to men, because it leaves men at the mercy of a woman's "feelings" and not common sense, and the facts.

Men shouldn't be put into a position to where they have to prove their innocence by default. We live in an equal society where everyone is considered innocent until proven guilty, not make anyone prove that they didn't do a crime. The question now is, what would be a fair check and balance in these cases because there's something wrong with this system in my view.

196

To me it has to be something that can be repeated. Something that she can document and prove that he repeatedly asked her out and that she rejected him repeatedly also. Not a one and done situation like in the story I just gave.

What do you think? Do you believe sexual harassment is when a person asks someone out "one" time and then that person deserves to lose their job over it? That sounds crazy to me. However, it may sound logical to others. But for those of you who believe he deserved it, be careful what you say because next time this can very easily be you. That's weaponizing sex. Men beware—there a price to pay.

Sexual harassment is a big thing in the workplace. It's very serious. Therefore, we have to make sure that the accusing mechanism is not abused and used against men as some form of anger management. We as a society have to have checks and balances in order to keep everyone fair and honest, including women.

I once talked to a woman who told me that she had a guy charged with sexual harassment at her job. She told me that this guy would make sexual jokes, not to her but while talking on the phone to his friends and buddies. She was walking by his cubicle and overheard a snippet (but not all) of the conversation. She said that she had gone to Management to file a complaint of sexual harassment against him.

I asked if she talked to him first about the situation. She said no because she doesn't want him to know that she was the one who complained. I said, why not? She said because he was a good guy and she didn't want him to be upset at her. I said that didn't make any sense to me; why couldn't she tell him so that he can stop it or keep his voice down because others hear him? I said at least give him a chance to correct the problem or situation. She said that she didn't think about that, she just knew it was offensive to women. I said, "but he wasn't talking to you or any other woman at your job, so how is this sexual harassment to you?"

Then she said it was because "I'm a woman and he shouldn't be talking about women that way." I said, "well, who are you, the 'judgment police? So, you get to determine who is harassed and who was not, even though it wasn't you and you had nothing to do with the situation?" She said that as long as he is denigrating women, then he is offensive towards all women. I said to her, "so you are going to try and get the guy fired and ruin his family and his life, just because you over heard s snippet of a conversation which had absolutely nothing to do with you?

She said that it was offensive to women and he shouldn't be offending women. I said, "what if it were your husband or boyfriend and some woman did the same thing to him, how would you feel about that?" She looked at me with a dumbfounded look in her face. Silence. I said, "enough said!" And left it at that.

To me this was women abusing the use of sexual harassment allegations as some kind of anger management. I don't know how some of you feel about this situation. Was this sexual harassment to you? What do you think? We have to have some kind of boundaries and standards for sexual harassment allegations otherwise we are setting a very dangerous precedent, because there are going to be a lot of men who don't want to work with or around women and may not want to hire them because of the fear of unreasonable views of sexual harassment. Now some of you may believe that this is reasonable.

So, let me ask you a question. What if it happens to you? Where somebody takes a small part of your conversation and reports it to management to get you fired? And what if they misinterpreted and misunderstood your conversation because they didn't hear it all or didn't know the context it was in? How would you feel now? I'm sure you would feel quite different now that it's your head on the chopping block. But when someone else in in the hot seat, no due process is okay, right?

This is why we have to draw clear cut lines so that people's "feelings" aren't the only basis to life affecting decisions. To me the aforementioned example clearly showed an abuse of power. Power that any woman can use against a man, and that's unfair, because it's unchecked, unchallenged and unbalanced! This was a woman weaponizing her sex (gender). Men—there's a price to pay!

CHAPTER 24

PORN, PROSTITUTION & STRIPPERS

The Women Who Sell Sex and
The Price of Admission
Selling sex-Who's in charge?

Porn, prostitution, and strippers all engage in sex for money. Why would a woman have sex and sell her body for money? The answer is, either she needs the money to take care of her lifestyle , that includes paying rent, taking of her children or school tuition and so on, and or a drug habit that she may have or she may just enjoy sex, e.g. a nympho, and likes getting paid in the process. These are the reasons a woman may have sex for money. Some of you maybe be asking yourself, "so what's wrong that? A woman can do whatever she wants, because it's her body."

That's true, she can do whatever she wants but there are

societal consequences for her actions. One of the consequences is that she will lose all respect from family, friends and others who see her engaging in that profession. Secondly, she is at risk of attracting a STD, meaning sexually transmitted disease for herself and others that she has sex with. Third, if she ever decides to change careers, her past will come back to haunt her.

For example: nobody would want to hire a woman with a checkered past like that as a schoolteacher or some other respectable profession like sales or any position dealing with the public. Why not? Because she would be an embarrassment to the company. Think about it, if a client was buying a something from her, as the salesperson, and then they remembered her face in a porn video, they just may not buy that product from her. Which means that the company will lose money in a sale but also she would give that same company a bad name with negative reviews if that information got out that the company was hiring porn stars to come into your house, around your kids selling products.

That's not a good look for the company. She would hurt their business. Therefore, why take a risk of bringing negative consequences to their business? What if she gets into a business which primarily works with kids? I'm quite sure that a lot of parents wouldn't want her around their kids as a moral issue. Also, what if she has kids and her kids' friends see her on a porn site or on the streets selling her body, how would her kids feel her then? I'm quite sure it would embarrass them, and it would change their view of their mother forever. They may not want to be part of her life in the future.

There are consequences for this type of lifestyle that these kinds of women engage in. These women are in charge, because it's their bodies. They are the sexual gatekeepers, which means that they can't blame anybody but themselves for the negative situations and consequences that they face in life, because all sexual decisions go through them. If you didn't believe me at this point that women are the sexual gatekeepers then explain how a woman, who wasn't forced, could sell her body for sex? It's because women are in charge of all sexual activity, including negative sexual activity.

Now you may be saying to yourself that some women are forced into prostitution, porn, or sex trafficking and that's against their will so it's not a choice and they are not in charge or in control. That's right, however I qualified that earlier in the book by saying that women are in charge and in control of all sexual activity, except in the case of forced sexual assault or abuse or any sexual activity that goes against their will.

However, saying that a woman has no choice but to sell her body to feed her children is not true. That career is not something that's forced on her, that's a choice she made. She could have gotten a job at McDonald's or to clean houses or something that didn't require a higher skill level or education. So, let's not try to make excuses for negative behavior, especially when these same women are in charge of the sexual activity that they engage in.

CHAPTER 25

SEXUAL MORALITY

Low Self Esteem-No Self Respect

Sexual morality means different things for different people. For some people it's their religion that leads them and they follow the moral grounds of that religion. For other people their self-respect and dignity are what's most important to them. And for others it's just common sense that drives morals. And for some, it's all of the above. And some people just don't have morals, anything goes for them. Sexual morals are a must in our society because otherwise we would have social chaos.

Why? Because, those who don't have morals would do all kinds of immoral things. Those people would make it okay for them to have sex with children, to create and engage in child porn and other disgusting behaviors that comes with having no morals. Also, they would have sex with animals. Sexual morals are what keeps men from having more than one wife at a time. Otherwise, if we had an immoral society there would be no honor or faith in people and that would be simply chaotic.

We have to trust someone otherwise we will trust no one. Sexual morals for people who are led by their religions or faith, see their body as a temple and they wouldn't let anybody violate them sexually. They will wait until they are married before they have sex with anyone. The women who use common sense for their morals will be very responsible when they have sex. They will use protection and have sex with one person at a time; they will never have multiple sex partners at the same time because they have self-respect and will not let a man turn them into a *whore*. Sexual morals come in different types of people with different types of mind sets.

For example: a woman who sells her body for money and gifts has no morals. Why? Because she doesn't give a damn about herself or who violates her most intimate space. She has no self-respect. Which means that her body doesn't mean anything to her if she is willing to give it up to anybody that has the dollars to pay for it. She's no better than a yard sale, selling junk and scraps for cash because that's the value she has put on her body parts.

Unfortunately, many of today's women who have multiple sex partners are no better. How? For the same reason. Why? Because if she is willing to spread herself around to multiple guys then where is her worth? Her value has dropped because she is used goods. It's like a used car. A used car does not have the same value as a new car. Why? Because too many drivers have misused it and wore it out and ran it down. That's how a woman body is when she lets every Tom, Dick and Harry use her body like a rental car. By the time someone decent comes along and wants to marry her, she is tired, old and wore out and really doesn't want to have sex a lot because she has had so many penises that she is sick of them. Therefore, the man is S.O.L., meaning *shit out of luck* because he can't enjoy his wife sexually because she has been broken down and wore out.

I know some women are saying that's not true. Okay, then explain why men say that as soon as they say, "I do" in marriage, then right after that the woman says "I don't", in that she "don't" want to have sex a lot. The majority of men who get married have the same story. Why? Because the women want to settle down now and take it easy because her body is tired and worn out due to the number of sex partners that she has had but doesn't tell him about. Therefore, since the man can't enjoy his wife sexually because she is tired of having sex and it's just not that important to her anymore because she has had her fill, he will cheat on her with another woman because she is not putting out and having sex with him, and because he has to get it from somebody. Believe it or not!

Therefore, her immoral behavior has indirectly cost her her marriage because the top thing that couples fight about and break up over is sex, and the other is money. I know some women will still say, "no, that's not it" and they will give a lot of excuses, like it's work or that they just don't have time anymore. If that's true and that's was the case, then how did they find time to have lots of sex before they got married? Why weren't they tired *before* they got into a relationship when they were having casual with multiple other guys?

Hmmm, sounds kind of strange that they had plenty of time to have sex with multiple partners before they got married but somehow, it's different because they are married. Makes no sense. And if it makes no sense, then it's not true. Could it just be that these women have just lost interest and sex is overrated, old and they are tired of it? Tired, because they have had so much sex with so many guys? I'm quite sure they won't admit that to their husband.

So, they give a thousand reasons why they can't have sex like they used too. But the reality is that they had low morals, and because they have had sex with multiple guys now their bodies are worn out and tired and it doesn't function like it used too. This is why women should have sexual morals and save their bodies for that special person who they want to spend the rest of their lives with long term rather than trying to be like a man and have casual sex with multiple sex partners and burning out their bodies up to the point where sex is no longer important to them anymore because they have had their fill.

Good luck in getting a man to stay in a sexless relationship with you, because you had no morals and ruined your sex life long-term. I know some women will say that they have to have sex while they are young and enjoy their youth. Sure, but they don't have to have multiple sex partners at one time. That's where the burn out comes from. Remember, too much of anything is poison. And too much sex is toxic and will cause women's bodies to burn out when that special person comes along. I guarantee it!

We have too many examples of forty-year-old women who just don't have the drive to have sexual regularly and that's because they have poisoned their bodies by having too much sex with too many men at the same time. Morals will give women longevity, and immorality will give women sexual burnout.

I must ask a question. Why would a woman treat the most sacred part of her body, the place where life begins, like a piece of trash? Having many men to denigrate and reduce her to a piece of ass with no value? It is her vagina that defines her as a woman. Her vagina defines her as a mother. Her vagina defines her as a wife or girlfriend. Her vagina defines her value and worth. Her vagina defines and enhances her beauty. Her vagina defines the respect that she commands and demands. Her vagina populates the world. Her vagina defines the most sacred place on this earth. Her vagina is a necessity that men can't do without. Her vagina is the most sacred space and place because mankind, *life itself,* would die out and become extinct without it.

So with as much value as her vagina has, I say again, why would a woman treat the most sacred part of her body, the place where life begins, like a piece of trash, by polluting the womb of life with all the different men ejaculating in her and using her vagina and discarding it like toilet paper? I know it sounds gross and disgusting (because it is) but that's the reality of the situation. Everybody wants to sugarcoat things in order to make it look good to justify their immoral behavior. This is why we need to return to our sexual morals!

ABOUT THE AUTHOR

K. B. Lewis was born in Mobile, Alabama, and grew up in Detroit, Michigan. He graduated from High School in Milwaukee, Wisconsin. He joined the U.S Navy in the mid 80's and moved to Northern California and was Honorably Discharged. He got married while in the military at the age of 20, and the marriage lasted for 13 years. He graduated from Unilex College in San Francisco, California with a degree in Business. He then moved to Memphis, Tennessee in the early 90's and then to Chicago, Illinois where he resides today.

www.kerryblewis.com

www.ingramcontent.com/pod-product-compliance
Lightning Source LLC
Chambersburg PA
CBHW031511040426
42445CB00009B/175